THAT LEADER IS YOU

RAHUL VASISHT

notionpress .com

INDIA · SINGAPORE · MALAYSIA

Notion Press

Old No. 38, New No. 6
McNichols Road, Chetpet
Chennai - 600 031

First Published by Notion Press 2019

ISBN 978-1-64587-738-7

To my parents,
For always loving and supporting me.
To my wife, Ritu,
For keeping up with my madness.
And, of course, Rajveer and Yuvraj,
Just so that the two boys know:
Papa loves you more than your mom.

Contents

Section 2

At the very onset, I am extremely grateful to all the individuals for agreeing to be a part of this book. I truly appreciate your kind help and am greatly humbled by the time and effort you have taken to help me compile your most valuable thoughts, ideas and suggestions. I, on my part, am hopeful; your contributions will go a long way in inspiring and motivating the entrepreneur and business leader of the future. For all your support and encouragement, I will remain ever thankful.

From the Author

In essence, each individual is a qualified entrepreneur and yet to be discovered business leader. For me, an entrepreneur will always remain more important than a business leader; there remains that undeniable truth that all business leaders once began their journey as simple, foolish and idealistic entrepreneurs. Perhaps the most essential truth that persists even today is that the majority of entrepreneurs will never achieve the heights required to be recognised as a business leader in the field of their preferred occupation and livelihood. This then raises the question as to what those habits, practices, behaviours and attributes are which allow a common entrepreneur to emerge as a leader of great consequence and significance with the passage of time.

My book titled 'That Leader is You' is divided into two sections: The first section is my humble attempt to identify and showcase those 12 habits, practices, behaviours and attributes which, in my opinion, are the basic necessities that an entrepreneur must possess in order to achieve the status of a business leader in the field of their operation. Furthermore, it is my endeavour to invite my readers on a journey to explore and investigate the entire gambit of my modest submission within an organisation setup. I frankly admit that the choice of investigating entrepreneurship and leadership in a business organisation is intentional and on purpose. In my opinion, the true test of individuals only comes to the forefront when they are put in situations which require them to both react and adapt to the human aspects within the business environment.

In the second section of my book, I have presented interviews with 10 different leaders in various fields. It has been my endeavour to introduce the reader to the various challenges that these individuals have faced and the methods they have employed to overcome and triumph over each adversity in their respective fields. I sincerely hope that the answers that these leaders have provided will inspire, motivate and encourage the reader on a journey of self-realisation that they themselves hold the keys to their success. Through the chapters presented in my book, I wish to make the readers discover that they already possess all that is required for them to become entrepreneurs and business leaders in their own right. It is for them to look within themselves and realise that the leader that they have searched for all this time to inspire and motivate them exists within them already, now and forever more!

That Leader is You!

Section 1

Chapter One

Belief in Self

"Believe you can
and
You're halfway there."

Theodore Roosevelt
(Former President of the United States of America)

This one inclination is by far one of the most essential attributes that individuals aspiring to become entrepreneurs and business leaders must cultivate within themselves. No one in this world is there to install the confidence a person needs to succeed, so, sorry, get used to it. You, yourself, must find a way to do it. In the simplest form, belief in self is a direct barometer of how one person perceives himself or herself. The advantage of this perception is that you possess the means to effect change first within yourself, then within others and, lastly and most importantly, transmit this change into the global consciousness. Only by believing in one's own abilities and strengths can a person make the necessary changes within themselves to achieve success both in their personal and professional life.

Identify This Leader

This leader was born to immigrant parents on the 6th of July 1946 in the city of New York. He was unable to complete his graduation after college due to his family's weak financial condition. He then decided to pursue his dream of acting. He was determined; he never refused any audition and attended screen test after screen test but met with failure every time. This led him to turn to writing scripts and screenplays so as to make ends meet. He eventually began to get minor roles, but these were mostly uncredited parts where he received limited screen appearances. It was in the year 1974 that he was finally able to land a role as one of the leads in a movie. Though this movie failed to be a success, it did secure him his first credit as a dialogue writer. The struggles did not end there, leaving him in a position where he became desperate to such an extent that he even had to pawn his wife's jewellery to provide the basic amenities for himself and his family.

One day, while watching a boxing match between the legendary Muhammad Ali and Chuck Wepner on television, he became inspired to write a script. He spent over 20 hours continuously writing and finally finished the script of the movie of an Italian boxer by the name of 'Rocky Balboa'; the title of the movie was 'Rocky'.

Such was his conviction in the quality of that just-written script that he right away started to market his manuscript to numerous film producers and movie studios. His only demand was that he should play the lead character, Rocky Balboa. And as always was the case, this was the demand that no producer or production company would ever agree to. He was regularly offered vast sums of money for the written script, yet he adamantly and voraciously refused to sign over the rights for the movie unless his demand of playing the lead was fulfilled. He fell into more difficult times; such was his desperation that he even sold his dog for a paltry sum of $50. It devastated him to do that. The offers still continued to flow from various directions for his magical script. At one point in time, the offer reached as high as $400,000 and yet he did not give up on his demand. He believed he was not a writer but an actor and the only person capable of playing the main role.

In the end, he accepted an offer of only around $25,000 for the script, but he had finally secured the role of Rocky Balboa. The movie went on to be released in the year 1976 as the much acclaimed 'Rocky'. The movie received 10 nominations from the Academy Awards, including one for best actor. It went on to win the awards for the best picture, best direction and best film editing respectively. The movie did a business of $225 million and eventually had seven sequels. As of 2015, the total aggregate of the entire series at the box office is estimated at over $1 billion. Our friend the actor, through his self-belief, is today credited as an actor par excellence, scriptwriter and film director. He now has a personal net worth of $400 million. Truly a rags-to-riches story!

So, were you able to identify this leader? You guessed it: Sylvester Stallone.

The above true story is self-explanatory. Read it and utilise it in the best way you see fit. Realise within yourself that it is only you who can make a change in your life. Life is not always good to all of us, but neither is life all bad to everyone. We have all had our share of success and failure. From the parts where you were successful, I say trust in yourself that you have the ability to make the correct decisions. As for the failures, ask yourself if they actually left you devastated, or did they make you stronger? The difference between success and failure is only when you decided to give up. I am sure you already know that, but how do we bring it into focus? To help you, I have listed some of the key elements below which will allow you to reacquire this focus. Remember that there is no exhaustive list in the world. I give you these to get yourself started on the right path to self-discovery.

Key Elements for Self-Belief

Focus on Past Achievements – 'Bhrama Astras'

No one will tell you this, but your past successes are your 'Bhrama Astras', and they serve only to remind you that if you were able to produce such amazing results in the past, there is no doubt that you will produce amazing results in the future.

Let your own past achievements inspire confidence in you, no matter who you are and at what stage you are in your life. I am yet to meet anyone without a few memories of excelling at some point in their personal and professional life. There will be many incidences where you excelled better than the competition—simple and small things such as doing well in a certain exam, winning either a school or college competition or making a brilliant presentation in your office.

These are your personal achievements; they have already happened. In almost all cases, you would have been nervous and doubtful before the final outcome. Use these experiences to confirm to yourself. **"I have been there, and I did really well."** Whenever that spectre of self-doubt appears in your mind, use the positive memories of the past to firmly defeat them.

Stop Comparing Yourself

This is perhaps the one habit that I blame our parents and elders for inculcating within us. This habit starts right from our childhood. First, it a comparison between the neighbourhood children or children at school, and if you have a sibling, then this comparison goes through the roof. Let me be categorical at this time and assure you: everyone has gone through it and, more importantly, it continues well into our adult life. The key difference is that it was a close family member who compared us first and now we regularly find reasons to do it to our own selves—simply, and incorrectly, comparing our accomplishment with the achievements of the other people around us, whether that is in the vicinity we reside or, as is most often the case, in our workplace.

Believe in your uniqueness. Have we really looked at ourselves in the mirror? Go on, indulge me. We all have many similar physical traits as our birth parents, but we look unique in our own way. If we look different from our own parents, then would it be wrong to say that we look completely different from other people throughout the world? Then, believe me, it's perfectly alright to be completely different from the whole wide world. It is because that is the natural course of things. Everyone is special, everyone is different. It is our diversity and combination of thought processes which make the world a unique place. There was one Mahatma Gandhi, there was one Albert Einstein, there is one Bill Gates, there is one Mahindra Singh Dhoni and there is only one Amitabh Bachchan. There is also only one of you, and the world waits for your unique contribution. All you have to do is believe it.

Help Someone

This is a wonderful exercise. Go out of your way to help someone. Please note I did not say help anyone who is less fortunate than you. The next time one of your friends, relatives or acquaintances asks you for help in any matter, something which requires you to help them with something only you can do, do it. I know a question has just gone up in your mind; I clarify I do not mean monetary help. The help should require you to, foremost, spend time doing it and thereafter it must not lead to any type of gain for your personal self.

This, in my experience, has a twofold effect on our self-belief. First, you should realise that the primary reason you have been approached for such help is that the other person believes in your ability to do so. It is, of course, an entirely different story if you don't believe in your own ability. The help you provide will, in turn, help you realise that there are indeed many qualities that are unique to yourself and thus it is you who should believe in your special set of skills. The confidence you are lacking is because you perceive yourself as not being good enough. Change this NOW.

Second, whenever we help someone, it allows us, for a brief moment of time, to walk in their shoes. More importantly, it gives us the ability to understand life from their perspective. In my experience, it reveals that they too have their unique strengths and weakness. They also have their fears of failure. So, you should be sufficiently confident that everyone at one point in their life has had self-doubt. Volunteering to help should make you count your blessings and further make you realise that you are not doing too bad for yourself. It was, in fact, only you who did not realise this.

So, just start by simply helping someone, without the desire for personal gain. This one benevolent act, the first of many, I hope, will help you to understand that the true story or their struggle is hidden from you. It is always imperative to appreciate and be thankful for all that you have in your life.

Work on Your Outward Appearance

In two scientific studies conducted in 2006, it was discovered that it takes the average human being only about one-tenth of a second to form the first opinion about the person they meet for the very first time. In fact, a scientific study as recent as 2014 implies that these first impressions are usually extremely accurate. Basically, even before we start speaking, the people we meet for the very first time are already assessing us. It should come as no surprise that first impressions count.

In fact, there are two human senses that play an active part; they are sight and smell. Spend time on your appearance, not money. Being well dressed and smelling good are instant self-image boosters. I have always observed that each individual defines their own style and concept for different professional and social events. Dressing well makes you feel more confident. The more confident you feel translates into more success. And, above all else, dressing well defines the person you are. You become your own self-advertisement poster. It's as simple as that.

Parting Advice: It's Alright to be Selfish

Live your life for yourself. Don't be afraid to take decisions because of what others say. Recognise for yourself who you are and what you want to be, then start working on it one small step at a time. Promise yourself to do only one thing differently every day. The results will surprise you. Stand up for what you believe is correct. Remember, it is always easier to convince others of your views when you first believe in them. As I said earlier, there is no exhaustive list. The key elements above have and are continuously being used by some of the most successful people in the world. I am sure that they will help you as well. Your self-belief will be a direct result of you investing time and effort in improving yourself. Find what works for you. I am sure whatever solutions you find on your road to becoming a more self-confident individual will be just as unique and exceptional as you are.

Chapter Two

Setting Realistic Goals

"A dream is just a dream.
A goal is a dream with a plan
and a deadline."

Harvey MacKay
(Businessman, Author & Columnist)

All successful people, irrespective of the field they are in, believe in setting goals for themselves. It is important to realise that goal setting is only the first step of a long process. I perceive it as answering the age-old question: **Where am I now and where do I want to be in the future?** Long story short, if you want to succeed, you need to set goals.

It is prudent to give careful consideration to how the set goal is going to be achieved. It must lead to a specific purpose and should be achieved within a definite time period. In my opinion, it is always a good practice to break up a long-term goal into many smaller, short-term objectives. Furthermore, each short-term objective must contain some very well-defined steps which are special and unique to the said short-term objective. It is a well-established tradition that it is the achievement of the short-term goals which eventually leads to the achievement of the ultimate goal. Please remember it is not important whether your goal is small or big. Ultimately, it is the planning and action that you undertake which will lead to the fulfilment of that goal. Some goals will take a day, some a few days, others a few years and, in some rare cases, even a lifetime.

Bhag Milkha Bhag: Goal Setting and Achievement at its Best

In the year 2013, a wonderful movie by the name 'Bhag Milkha Bhag' was released. This movie was scripted by Prasoon Joshi, directed by Rakeysh Omprakash Mehra and had Farhan Akhtar in the lead role. Many believe it to be a biopic of perhaps India's greatest athlete Milkha Singh. It truly is a testament to one man's rise from poverty to his ultimately becoming a national treasure.

This movie had many inspirational parts in it; however, to better explain in the context of goal setting, I would like to draw your attention to the part of the movie where, due to his indiscipline while training for the Melbourne Olympics, he fails to qualify for the main event. He, on the return flight back to India, then proceeds to his coach and asks him for the current world record of the 400m race. His coach simply writes down the figure '45.8' on a paper napkin and hands it back to Milkha Singh. From that minute on, Milkha dedicates himself to the achievement of that one single goal. Such is his determination that he does not allow any sort of temptation or inducement to come in the way of his training till the time he equals and then breaks that record.

While it is important to commend him on achieving that goal, it is more pertinent to notice the planning that he employs to reach the ultimate achievement of his goal. Nothing else remains in his life but that single goal. How many of us clearly remember his physical appearance changing from a fit individual to a completely chiselled body! Furthermore, the scene of him emptying his soaking wet jersey in that empty bucket time and time again until the bucket is brimming to the top with his own sweat. In addition, the scene where is he seen refusing the advances of a female athlete with the words: "Forgive me, I am not insulting you, but I am in a battle within myself."

Moreover, when some time has elapsed and Milkha Singh goes for his next world tournament, you observe that while he is praying to god, the piece of paper with the figure '45.8' is in the same place in front of his eyes, always reminding him of his objective.

Now, what does the above passage teach us about goal setting?

Write Down Your Goals

Everyone, including myself, always speaks about what we want to achieve. However, I highly suggest you entrench yourself down and compose yourself; take a piece of paper and write down what your most important goal is. The reason behind writing down your goals is essential, because the minute you write things down, you effectively end up being more committed to achieving them. In fact, there have been many studies which suggest that people who write their goals down have a much higher chance of achieving them in comparison to those people who do not follow the practice of putting down their goals in a written format.

Make a Flexible Plan

Once you have written down your goal, it is important to figure out how you're going to get to it. For that, it becomes important to set up a plan. Now, it is important to remember that this plan is an initial plan, i.e. this plan should start you off on your journey towards the goal. However, always keep in mind that as situations change, so does your plan. New situations will arise, and you must adapt and mould yourself and the circumstances around you to achieve your goal.

Keep it in Front of You

Consistently reminding yourself of your goal is sometimes difficult. Don't worry, it's a very human trait. Keep an object close by, whether it be a piece of paper, a favourite quote, a photograph—it could be anything which reinforces your determination towards your goal. I assure you there will be times when you feel like giving up. It is at that time that keeping an object which reminds you of your goal will help you to remain steadfast as well as encourage you to continue to work towards achieving that set forth goal.

Set Smaller Goals to Get to the Larger Goal

It is essential to realise that goals take time to achieve and so you must be willing to spend the time in achieving them. One of the sure-shot ways of achieving your ultimate goal is to break it up into smaller goals. To put it more simply, imagine that you want to reach the fifth floor of a building; your journey starts at the ground floor. Visualise the voyage from the first floor to the fourth as the achievement of smaller goals. As you reach each floor, you get closer to your ultimate goal. This is the factual and accurate way of achieving your goal. Only by setting smaller targets and then achieving them will you be able to be in a position of fulfilling your desired ultimate goal.

Here, I would like to take the opportunity to introduce a goal-setting technique employed by some of the most successful large corporations, industrialists, entrepreneurs and business leaders throughout the world. This system is commonly referred to as the **S.M.A.R.T.** criteria and is an outstanding application with regard to goal setting. I truly believe that this system is easy to understand and, more importantly, easily applies to almost all situations in one's personal and professional life.

S.M.A.R.T. Criteria

George T. Doran is commonly attributed for the introduction of the S.M.A.R.T. criteria through a paper published in Management Review in the November 1981 issue under the title of 'There's a S.M.A.R.T. Way to Write Management's Goals and Objectives'. Doran recognised the need for companies to achieve their goals and targets. He was clear in emphasising that goals and targets are never vague or incoherent in nature, but in fact, they should be well structured, transmissible and measurable. It was with these objectives in mind that he was able to introduce the very first rational system of defining, communicating as well as setting up of a realistic time-bound frame to enable a company to achieve its ultimate objectives and targets.

In essence, any **S.M.A.R.T.** goal should have five elements. They are:

- **S**pecific.
- **M**easurable.
- **A**ttainable.
- **R**elevant.
- **T**ime-Bound.

Set Specific Goals

Specific means **"what needs to be done".** Your goal must be clear and even the final result must be predefined. Basically, you must be clear about what exactly you want. There is no place for being vague or causing any sort of confusion with what the goal is. More importantly, all the personnel or departments even remotely affected or involved must be clear about their job role and must always be made aware of the ultimate goal. Special care should be given to ensure that communication between all parties involved must be always encouraged.

It helps when you ask yourself certain questions such as:

Who: Who or which people are to be involved?

When: Establish a definite time frame.

Which: Identify the areas which are best suited or gain the most with regard to the goal.

Where: Identify a market or department or location where the goal will be ultimately utilised.

What: Special requirements or restrictions or alternatives needed for achieving the goal.

Why: The need to achieve such a goal.

All Goals Must be Measurable

A **measurable** goal means that there must be a way to either quantify or calculate a goal; it is mainly to help in evaluating how much we have progressed in achieving our goal. A simple example is when a person sets a target to lose weight, such as 20 kilograms in a period of 20 weeks. This measurable figure allows one to track how much they weigh at present (kilograms), how much weight they have targeted to lose and the period of time (weeks) they have calculated for the achievement of their target. Both the figures are quantified, but more importantly, the progress to lose the weight can be precisely tracked.

It helps when you ask yourself certain questions such as:

How much?

How many?

Without a suitable way to measure your success, you miss out on the opportunity that comes with knowing what you have actually achieved and how much is yet to be accomplished.

Set Attainable Goals

The world **"attainable"** means realistic. I repeat, practical. Many large and super successful personalities and companies have fallen prey to failure by setting totally unrealistic goals for themselves. This means no outlandish or implausible ideas, i.e. if you set a goal that you have little or no hope of achieving, it will lead you to failure, and in most cases, it will also lead to loss of reputation for both the individual or the organisation in question. Therefore, the prerequisite for an attainable goal is that it must always be an achievable goal.

This brings me to also inform you that an attainable goal does not mean that you set yourself an easy goal. The essence of a goal is that it must be challenging and lead to quantitative rewards both for the individual and organisation. Remember: if you set yourself an easy goal, you may have inadvertently already failed even before you have started. You must realise that the goals you set, and the steps you take on the road to achieving them, must be sensible and sustainable both in the short as well as in the long term.

Set Relevant Goals

When the word **relevant** is used, it means closely connected or appropriate to the achievement of the goal. This is basically a piece of advice that when the larger goal is broken down into smaller targets, those smaller targets must be concise and precisely related to the ultimate goal. Many a time the ultimate goals set up by an individual and an organisation have simply been lost because a new discovery or a new process diverts the attention and focus away from that which was set up to be achieved in the first place, resulting in disastrous effects. So, it is essential that the total focus must always be on the achievement of the ultimate goal. New processes or new areas of interest should only be pursued after the original goal is accomplished.

All Goals Must be Time-Bound

Goals and targets without deadlines tend to be put off until another day. All goals, personal or professional, will just not get done by themselves. For goals to be successful, an endpoint should be identified. It is essential to set up a reasonable yet specific date of completion for the goal. A commitment to a deadline helps both the individual as well as the team to focus their efforts on the completion of the goal on or before the due date. A time-bound goal will provide you with the crucial focus and sense of urgency to make it happen.

It helps when you ask yourself certain questions such as:

When?

Where do I need to be in a week?

Where should I be in three months, six months or even a year?

What can I get done today?

Please note: Some authors and management gurus have further added some additional criteria to the above introduced S.M.A.R.T. criteria. These new criteria, however, do not encroach much on the original criteria, but I am of the opinion that they certainly improve the original idea introduced by Doran in the year 1981. Here, I take the opportunity to introduce two such proposed improvements in the form of the S.M.A.R.T.E.R. criteria and the S.M.AR.T.E.S.T. criteria.

S.M.A.R.T.***E.R***., where E.R. may mean:

Evaluate and Review.

Enthusiastically and Rewards.

Ethical and Recorded.

Evaluate and Redo.

S.M.A.R.T.***E.S.T***., where E.S.T. may mean:

Energised, Stated and Take the first step.

Excited, Shared and Task-Oriented.

Evaluate, Support and Trust.

As you will notice, each of the new suggested improvements to the S.M.A.R.T. criteria has a different meaning and importance. This arises because of the use of these criteria by various professionals and organisations throughout the world. Each successful entrepreneur and business has adapted and adopted the criteria specific to their needs and requirements. Choose one which aligns best to your objectives and to your criterion.

In my personal capacity, I have always utilised the S.M.A.R.T. criteria, but I highly recommend to the reader that before they finally select a criterion, they should at least have a general knowledge of the other goals criteria available. This will allow the people concerned to choose a system most suited to their needs and requirements.

Chapter Three

The Skill of Negotiation

"In business as in life –
You don't get what you deserve,
You get what you negotiate."

Chester L. Karass
(Author & Negotiating Genius)

Organisations don't negotiate: people negotiate on behalf of the organisation. Negotiation is, in fact, a constant yet invisible part of our daily life. We unknowingly use this skill throughout our whole lives. We unsuspectingly use it even with our friends and family; therefore, it should come as no surprise that this skill of negotiation is also an essential key to business success. An effective negotiator is one of the most highly prized employees of an organisation. It is important to remember that no person is a born negotiator. The art of negotiation is learnt through personal experience, the pursuit of knowledge and, above all else, is an instinctive ability of constant problem-solving over a substantial period of time.

Negotiation in its simplest use is a method by which two or more parties settle each other's differences. All negotiations are based on the principles of mutual benefit and fairness. It is not a competition where the winner takes all, but it is essentially the formulation of an agreement by means of compromise and adjustment, which leads to an amicable outcome for all parties concerned. In any disagreement, the aim should be to achieve the best possible result. The negotiation space is not a stage for personal ego or insults or misbehaviour. In any given scenario, the objective is to work out a win-win situation, all the while maintaining a cordial relationship such that it transpires in both parties a feeling that they have been able to achieve some substantial gain from the just concluded negotiations.

The Theodore Roosevelt Presidential Photograph

Theodore Roosevelt, in the year 1912, decided to run a second time for the office of the president of the United States. His entire re-election campaign was being guided through an exceptional manager by the name of George Perkins, who had earlier served in the position of a partner in the business firm of J.P. Morgan. This election was probably one of the toughest and closely fought elections ever held for the presidential post. The campaign team of Theodore Roosevelt came up with the strategy that near the end of the campaign trail, they would distribute pamphlets with a printed speech of the former president, and the highlight of the said pamphlet would be a photograph of Theodore Roosevelt, which would appear on its cover. The belief was that such a distribution would not only highlight the new ideas of Theodore Roosevelt but would also give him great visibility as well as recall value in the mind of the voters.

To this effect, the campaign team printed around three million pamphlets. Once they were printed, but just before their distribution, it was discovered that no one had taken the permission of the photographer whose photo had been ultimately used on the pamphlet. To make matters worse, the copyright law in place at that time allowed the photographer the right to demand as much as $1 per copy per photograph. Simply put, in the year 1912, that would translate to a payment of three million dollars. That would mean a loss of three million dollars to the entire campaign, a loss that would be very difficult to recover from. Furthermore, the alternative was to have a reprint, which added to the financial loss and would also cause significant delays to the campaign trail.

Not able to come up with a suitable solution to their predicament, the problem was handed over to George Perkins. Such was the brilliance of the man that on being presented with the problem, he called in a stenographer to his office and dictated a letter to be sent to the photographer, which read: "We are planning to distribute three million copies of a campaign speech with the photograph of the former President Theodore Roosevelt. This presents an excellent opportunity for the photographer and studio whose photograph will be used. How much are you willing to pay to use your photographs? Respond immediately."

The reply of the photographer was almost instant and exceedingly prompt. His telegram in response to the letter sent by George Perkins read: "I appreciate the opportunity, but under current circumstances, I can only afford to pay you a sum of $250."

On his part, George Perkins immediately sent the amount to the photographer and thus the deal was sealed. The above-presented story is a prime example that sometimes in real-life negotiations it becomes important to think out of the box. Sometimes to find a solution, there exists no specific rule or framework for a satisfactory result.

However, it is essential to realise that all great negotiators have a regular habit of thinking systematically and strategically about negotiations. They take special care to prepare themselves to execute and achieve the best result successfully. The **not so envious** role of any negotiator is to come up with the **best solution** for the **worst problem** with the **smallest amount of information** at hand, with the **least resources** at his disposal, in the **shortest time** possible.

Through this chapter, I hope to introduce you to some of the most important and frequently utilised practices in real-life situations. The objective is to enable you to handle even the most difficult negotiations in a well-structured manner so as to allow you the opportunity to maximise your chances of success. I hope that they will help in your journey of becoming a master negotiator.

Research and Preparation

One of the most primary duties of a good negotiator is to research and prepare for the day of negotiation. This preparation is absolutely essential for the positive outcome of the negotiation. Good negotiators begin their preparation days in advance of the final day of the negotiation. It is better to put it as the first of many rounds of negotiations. In fact, the negotiators of both parties will spend substantial time and energy in determining how they will actually conduct themselves and their team during the period of the negotiations.

While it is common to pay attention to set forth goals, targets and purpose, it is more important to plan how the said ambitions of the company are met. To this effect, good negotiators will study each and every individual who will make up the other's negotiation team. Also, special emphasis will be placed on the history of the past relationships between the two parties to find areas of agreement and common goals. In addition, areas for trade-offs and alternatives to the stated goals will also be explored and exploited.

In negotiations, it helps to answer questions such as:

- What is it I really want to achieve?
- What are the areas which are unacceptable for negotiation?
- What am I willing to give away?
- What other options or alternatives are available?
- What kind of leverage can I utilise for my benefit?
- Am I bargaining from a position of strength or weakness?
- What are the other variables at play?
- What don't I know and how can I get the other team to reveal it to me?

Attentive Listening

All effective negotiators are attentive listeners. They allow all parties involved to speak their mind, all the while listening to them with great curiosity. Listening is not only a matter of importance, but it also conveys respect to the other parties involved. It is always a well-established practice that the more a negotiator listens, the more he is able to assess the sincerity and capacity of the other negotiating team. Listening well allows a person to gain a full understanding of the topic being discussed. More importantly, it allows the good negotiator to understand to a great extent the modus operandi which is being used and, as such, allows him to formulate counter suggestions to mould out the result of the negotiation in favour of himself and his team.

Verbal Communication

The next step for any good negotiator is to effectively communicate to the other side what he and his team believe are their points of discussion clearly. There is no space for any sort of misunderstanding during a negotiation. It is of paramount importance that a negotiator has the requisite skills to state his side of the discussion, and as such, this should be presented with sound reasoning and judgement. The objective of verbal communication is to convince the other side of the sincerity of the offer on the table and then to gently persuade for a mutually beneficial agreement.

Emotional Control

It is an endeavour of all good negotiators to control the tone of the negotiation. As I have stated earlier, the negotiation table is not a place for competition or putting the other party down. Every negotiator pays special attention to keep his as well as his team's emotions under control. As is in life, a single episode of an unwarranted emotional outburst leads to negations falling apart in most cases. The major downside to such an episode is that the other party may never return to the negotiation table ever again. This, in turn, would lead to a total breakdown of communication between the two parties. Furthermore, it would cause a great set back to the hard work put in for the preparation of the negotiation, which would invariably lead to delays and loss in financial terms to both parties. Negotiations must always be held in a cordial manner in an environment which is conducive to achieve the desired result of the negotiation.

Problem-Solving

One of the key attributes of a skilled negotiator is to always have alternative solutions. This stems from the fact that no matter how well a negotiator and his team prepare for discussion, there will sometimes be completely unimaginable obstacles to the success of the negotiations. It is at this point of time that the experienced negotiator will need to come up with an equally out of the box solution. In essence, a negotiator must solve each of the problems presented to him at the negotiation table, irrespective of how small or large the issue is at hand. His objective is and will always remain the fruitful conclusion of the negotiation, and that path will be achieved only through his ability of constructive problem-solving.

Teamwork = Joint Effort

Any negotiator is only as good as his team. The virtues of a good team cannot be elaborated enough. A team may be led by a negotiator, but it is important to realise that it is the team which prepares the negotiator. The strength of a team is formed by the diversity that each member brings to that team. Each member supports the other through his unique skill and insight at the negotiation table. In simple terms, when the negotiation is successful, it is the success of the whole team. It is always the entire team which is accredited for the win and not just the 'lead negotiator'.

Decision-Making Ability

I have used the term 'lead negotiator' to draw your attention to the fact that within a negotiation team, there is a well-structured hierarchy in place. One person is always empowered to make the final call on all decisions at the negotiation table. Sometimes, it is necessary to act decisively or agree to a compromise to achieve the desired results. It is best explained thus: While the credit of a successful negotiation is shared by the team, the responsibility of a failed or unsuccessful negotiation is always the fault of the lead negotiator.

Trust and Reliability

Finally, a good negotiator is renowned for his ability to keep his promise. A negotiator is duty-bound to stand by each of the clauses or points of agreement between the two parties. It is his personal integrity which is demonstrated when he not only takes what is due to him from the negotiating table but, more importantly, he delivers all that he had promised to the opposite side at the time of negotiations.

Three Important Concepts of Negotiation Theory

I would like to introduce you to three different concepts of negotiation theory here. These concepts are utilised in almost all situations in the real world. It is my firm belief that a good negotiator must have a fair idea of these concepts, as they are essential for success at the negotiating table.

B.A.T.N.A.

B.A.T.N.A. or **Best Alternative To a Negotiated Agreement** was a term first coined by Roger Fisher and William Ury in their 1981 bestseller, 'Getting to Yes: Negotiating Without Giving In'. In the simplest terms, BATNA is an alternative course of action that all parties should have in place if they fail to reach an agreement at the negotiating table. The correct use of the BATNA method allows a negotiating team to assess its strength at the negotiating table. It is a well-calculated strategy which allows one to realise how much pressure can be applied to the opposite negotiating team. A strong BATNA allows for a stronger position of negotiation and, in fact, directly affects which of the negotiating teams will have more influence and control over the proceeding of the negotiations.

Illustrative Example

Sean is looking to sell his second-hand car. He first approaches the dealer from who he has bought the car. That dealer offers him a guaranteed offer of Rs. 60,000. Sean then puts up an advertisement in the newspaper. Roger reads that advertisement and approaches Sean with a firm price of Rs. 55,000. Just as Sean is about to finalise the deal, his close cousin George approaches him with an offer of Rs. 65,000, but George can only pay him that amount 30 days from now.

So, now Sean has three alternatives:

a. Offer of the car dealer of Rs. 60,000.
b. Offer from Roger of Rs, 55,000.
c. Offer from George of Rs. 65,000; however, he would only receive that amount after a period of 30 days.

Now, Sean has the advantage of knowing that the highest price he can receive for his second-hand car is Rs. 60,000. He has two other firm offers in his hand; while the one from Roger is a lower offer of Rs. 55,000, the other from George of Rs. 65,000 is most definitely tempting. This offer from George, however, forces a trade-off between an extra gain of Rs. 5000 and the waiting period of 30 days. Therefore, now Sean must apply the BATNA concept to finalise the best deal from all the alternative offers presented to him.

In all three scenarios, there is one constant theme: You must have the ability to walk away from a transaction. He or she who cares least usually always wins. However, realistically, we have upper and lower limits to everything. The key is to really understand the upper and lower limits of the other party so you can get to as high and profitable a limit as possible without risking the possibility of the other side walking away from the negotiating table.

Z.O.P.A.

Z.O.P.A. or **Zone of Possible Agreement** is defined as the range of possible agreement within which negotiation can be concluded with mutual benefit to all parties.

The process of finding this zone requires some inputs of information. It begins with a proposal by a person or organisation that puts an offer on the negotiation table. The other party of the negotiation, whether that is a person or organisation, receives this offer and then considers the merits of the offer. Both parties are aware that there is always a scope of negotiation on that offer. This is referred to many times as the "bargaining range". Both parties are aware of their **Zone of Possible Agreement,** and in almost all cases where negotiations are successfully concluded, it is done both within that zone and range.

Illustrative Example

An organisation is looking to raise money through a term loan. To this effect, it approached three financial institutions. The current bankers (Bank A) to the organisation have already offered an interest rate of 10.25% per annum. The offers it has received from two other banks, B & C, are as below:

Bank A: An interest rate of 10.25% per annum.

Bank B: An interest rate of 10.15% per annum.

Bank C: An interest rate of 10.10% per annum.

After receiving all the offers from different banks, the organisation now approaches its current bankers for negotiating the final rate of interest. The current bankers also have made it abundantly clear that they would not like to break the relationship with the organisation. During the negotiations, the organisation asks for a rate of 9.90% per annum. The bank counters that offer with an offer of 10.10% per annum. Now, the ZOPA for both parties is between 10.25% and 9.90%, but the bargaining range is now changed and stands between 10.10% and 9.90%. During the negotiation, both parties mutually agree on a rate of 10.05% per annum; this is when the deal is finalised.

W.A.P.

W.A.P. or **Walk Away Price** is best defined as a reserve price. That is, in the case of both individuals and organisations in any deal, if the minimum price is not met, any of the two parties, whether buyer or seller, will exercise their right to walk away from the negotiation table. The reservation price differs for both buyers and sellers and is influenced by factors such as disposable income, desire to acquire or retain the said product and availability of substitute products in the market.

Illustrative Example

Timothy and company are art auctioneers. In their annual art auction, they have been able to convince the owner of a rare painting to offer that work for auction. The owner of the said painting has agreed to sell the painting only if he receives a minimum price of Rs. 100,000. This minimum price set by the owner of the painting is referred to as "reserve price". In the course of the auction, even with the best efforts of the auctioneers, no buyer offers the reserve price. Thus, the painting remains unsold.

This leads us to deduce three facts from the above illustration. First, the painting is a rare commodity, with hardly any substitute in the market. Secondly, the seller has set what he feels is his minimum requirement or "reserve price". Thirdly, the buyers at the auction, maybe due to the pressure of their disposable income, do not offer a price which matches the seller price. This leads the buyers to walk away from the auction, leading to the painting remaining unsold.

In conclusion, I have tried to introduce the reader to a few negotiation concepts, but it is important to realise that to become a great and reputed negotiator, it is always prudent to learn and study other negotiation concepts and case studies. I urge you to seek out these other concepts and real-life examples associated with the subject of negotiation to allow yourself to enhance and further develop your negotiating skills.

Chapter Four

Your Family Comes First... Always

"It didn't matter how big our house was;
It mattered that there was love in it."

Peter Buffett
(Musician and Author)

"No matter what you've done for yourself or for humanity,
If you can't look back on having given love and attention to your own family,
What have you really accomplished?"

Lee Iacocca
(President, CEO, Chairman – Chrysler 1978-1992)

For any entrepreneur or business leader, the new enterprise or business he sets up is like a newborn baby. And just as a newborn baby, this new enterprise also requires his undivided attention and time. In almost all cases, this comes at the cost of the time and attention which are rightfully due to his wife, children and other family members.

However, it is also interesting to note that almost all successful entrepreneurs, men and women alike, take out time from their schedules and dedicate it to spending time with their families. In fact, the most successful global business leaders credit their success to their secure home environment. In these cases, family members have taken up the responsibility of running the household, thus allowing the business entrepreneur to peacefully focus all their energy towards the running and growing of the business.

This chapter is dedicated to those aspects which allow for the formation of a supportive family structure, and more importantly, it highlights those facets which all true successful entrepreneurs should adopt, which I am hopeful will contribute to the creation of a supportive home environment. Through this chapter, I wish to salute the sacrifices made by members within the family. They may not be involved in running the business, but in most cases, their contribution both to the individual's and the organisation's success is unrivalled and beyond compare.

Sudha Murthy and Narayan Murthy: Sacrifice of a Wife

Mr Narayan Murthy, one of the founders of Infosys, which is one of the largest and most successful software companies of the world, has always credited his wife, Sudha Murthy, as one of the pillars of his success. Narayan Murthy and Sudha Murthy were introduced to each other through a common friend in Pune. At this early stage of his life, Narayan Murthy had no intentions of going into business for himself. In fact, he wanted to join politics and also wanted to set up and run an orphanage. Mrs Sudha Murthy, on the other hand, at this time, was already a trailblazer in her life. She was one of the first female employees at a Tata firm, that too on the factory work floor.

After having spent considerable time together, mainly spent by watching movies and going out to relatively low-priced restaurants, where they followed the Dutch system (each one paid their share of the bill amount) of paying all the bills, as there was a substantial difference between both their incomes. Yet, love blossomed and Mr Narayan Murthy finally proposed marriage to Sudha Murthy, that too in an auto rickshaw. His proposal went something like this, "I am 5'4" tall, my circumstances and ambitions are not hidden from you. I can never hope to give you great riches, but I promise to give you a happy and comfortable life. You are an intelligent and beautiful woman, and you can have any man you like. But I would like to marry you. I hope that you will accept my proposal." While Sudha Murthy did not answer at that time, she promised to get back to him.

When she did break the news of the proposal to her parents, her father rejected the idea outright. Thus, their relationship continued this way for another three years, but eventually, the couple were able to convince their families and were married in the year 1978. The marriage was a simple affair, which was held in the presence of their parents at Narayan Murthy House. The total cost of the marriage was Rs. 800, and as always, both Narayan Murthy and Sudha Murthy split the expenses and paid the bill by going Dutch.

It was in the year 1981 that Narayan Murthy decided he wanted to start a software company in the name of 'Infosys'. This time, the vision was there, but the finances were not in place. This time also, it was Sudha Murthy who decided to support the dream of her husband and gave him Rs. 10,000, which she had saved up over a large period of time. She was firm in her belief that she would handle the responsibility of running the household and allow Narayan Murthy to follow his dream of setting up his new enterprise.

It is important also to know that in the early days, both Narayan and Sudha Murthy contributed to the birth and growing of Infosys. Narayan Murthy was very clear that he clearly disapproved of a husband and wife combination at the office. This decision of Narayan Murthy left Sudha Murthy shocked. It was much later, by her own admission, that she realised that when an individual is out to set up a brand-new enterprise, he must remain 100% focused and committed to the organisation; thus, if both husband and wife remain within the organisation, their family and children would eventually suffer. It was for the well-being of the family and her household that Sudha Murthy sacrificed her career, a decision which she has never regretted, and it is a fact that her husband, Narayan Murthy, has always appreciated and highlighted.

In his own words, he always affirms, "Sudha, I stepped on your career to make mine. You are responsible for my success."

From the above true story, it is evident that Narayan Murthy was well aware of the fact that if both he and his wife were involved in the new enterprise, the enterprise would be successful, but the family would suffer. Therefore, in the interest of their family, he put his foot down, and when Sudha Murthy realised the noble intention of her husband, she also sacrificed her ambitions for the betterment of the family. This should make one realise that it is because the home environment was firmly secured that Narayan Murthy, the entrepreneur, was able to become a grand success.

While the above presentation has only highlighted the role of the wife and her sacrifice towards the success of her husband, there are many amazing stories around the world of the sacrifices made by various members of the family. These sacrifices have ultimately led to the success of the entrepreneur in their chosen field of expertise. Essentially, a successful leader devotes time outside the business towards his family. It is never about the money or the gifts or the parties. It's all about giving your family your precious time. It is all about building and reinforcing the bonds within the family. It should, therefore, come as no surprise that almost all entrepreneurs and business leaders find some simple yet innovative ways of spending time with their family.

I have presented below some of the easiest ways entrepreneurs and business leaders can and should spend quality time with their family members.

Don't Miss the Milestones

Children are an important part of every family. Once your work has ended, dedicate the time available to your children, just as you have to your company. The most successful of entrepreneurs and business leaders alike schedule their children into their lives. Though the word 'schedule' may seem severe in its use, it also shows that time spent with children is an essential ingredient in the success of the business. Numerous times, there are special events, such as sports day, drama day or any competition, in which a child will participate. Make it a point to be there; these are the only memories that a child holds in his heart. In fact, even while you're reading this, do you, the reader, not remember an event that you wish that your parent or parents had been a part of, but due to some unavoidable reason, they could not be part of that event? You regret that even now, don't you? I know I have some events like those as well. Don't miss the important milestones of your children. They may seem insignificant to you, but you being a part of it means the world to them.

Eat Your Meals Together

One of the greatest opportunities within any family is to catch up over a family meal. In our family, it was almost always dinner. In almost all the autobiographies I have read about great leaders, whether they are in business or any other field, there is always a mention of the family having one meal together. The time which is spent over a meal is a great time to unwind from the worry of the office. It is a time to catch up on the happenings of the day, the small victories, to help each other with certain issues which may have arisen during the day. It is a time to laugh and joke and enjoy each other's company. In fact, it is the best time for the entrepreneur to appreciate the hard work of the wife and the children during the day, thus, in turn, allowing for the creation of a safe and comfortable environment where matters may be discussed and solved. This one small event of sharing a meal together promotes a great sense of belonging within the family and helps to strengthen the bonds of the intrapersonal relationships and associations within a family.

Switch Off Hour of the Day

There is no denying it, we are a slave to our electronic systems, whether that is to the television, the computer or the cell phone. Admit it, a vast majority of us are addicted to the electronic and information highway. While it is acceptable that we use these formats very aggressively in our workspace during the day, there is no excuse for continuing their use when most of us reach the warm confines of our home. Many successful entrepreneurs and business leaders follow the practice of limiting their own and their family members' access to electronic devices such as the computer, the television and the use of cellular phones once they are home. This type of curfew usually extends for maybe an hour or much longer. This time is meant for the whole family to catch up with each other and share between themselves how their day was spent. Doing this for just one hour every day results in an exceptional bonding between each of the members of the family. I highly recommend that this should be followed; the results are simply too remarkable to illustrate through writing.

Plan All Family Holidays at the Beginning of the Year

I highly recommend this habit to all my friends and acquaintances. In fact, I first heard of this kind of planning when I had an opportunity to catch a television interview of Indra Nooyi, the president and chief operating officers of one of the largest beverage companies of the world. She clearly stated that she always marked out her holidays with the family at the beginning of the financial year. She also made sure that that the dates she marked in the calendar were well circulated to those who were the key officials in her organisation. The net result of doing this was that she as well as her team knew that any or all work needed to be finished by the time she went on vacation, failing which the unfinished work would be completed when she came back from her holiday. This is a classic case where a business leader acknowledges her family as a priority and finds a way to achieve a balance between her professional and personal life. Family vacations are an important time both for the children and the spouse, and everyone should schedule and plan them well in advance.

Be Spontaneous

Not everything in life can be planned; sometimes it's better to go with the flow. Doing activities such as going for a walk, watching a movie or even sharing a household chore, riding bikes, hiking, going swimming, going to a museum—the list is endless—leads to bonding with family. It's all about being in the present. How many of us can deny the fact that sometimes, more often than not, we get off early from work?

However, how many of us are guilty of then coming back to our home and then just wasting our time in front of the television? Don't deny it; we all are guilty of doing the same. Now, just imagine if we spent that same time playing with the children or helping our spouses with a household chore. It's all about living at the spur of the moment and being impulsive. These unplanned moments are some of the most cherished by any family. Don't believe me? Try it and find out.

Family Hug Time

No matter how busy your schedule is during the day, there is always time to hug your family and tell them that you love them. Hugging your family reinforces the feeling that they are more important to you than your work. It promotes a feeling of well-being and strengthens the belief that they are the centre of your universe. I have seen that some parents feel awkward to hug their children publicly. I have often approached such parents to ask why they feel that way. I can tell you that I am yet to receive a satisfactory answer.

Another uncomfortable situation I have encountered is that most parents feel afraid of saying those three magic words—I LOVE YOU—to their spouse and their children. Saying or telling your family members that you love them should always be an exceedingly simple and natural process. In simple terms, sometimes each and every one of us needs to hear the words, and it is not enough to be satisfied with saying that it is always implied. In fact, if an individual cannot be himself or herself in front of his or her own spouse and children, I genuinely wonder where else they are able to be themselves.

Be Available

It is very important for family members to believe that their entrepreneur father or mother is easily available to them. This is usually achieved by securing their belief that they are only a phone call away. I realise that sometimes it is difficult to pick up the phone at that instant. However, steps must be taken so as to make them rest assured that once it is possible, you will call back. Simply put, sometimes your coming on the line, even for a brief conversation, means a great deal to all your family members.

In conclusion, it is important to realise that all successful entrepreneurs and leaders, whether they be men or women, are human. They are also intimately bound by their relations to their family. While there is no denying that it is their enterprise or organisation which needs a large part of their time and focus, the importance of family and the cultivation of close family ties are also paramount. It is an essential and irrefutable responsibility of each entrepreneur and leader to strike a healthy balance between work and family. What is the point of earning all the money in the world and having no one to share it with at the end? I firmly believe that no matter what the circumstances may be, each and every one has the ability to keep their connections with their families. In the end, it is only about what is more important. I encourage you to answer this question for yourself. The answer will, I hope, encourage you to realise the importance of your family in your own life.

Chapter Five

The Importance of Decision Making

"I don't believe in taking right decisions,
I take decisions and make them right."

Ratan Tata
(Chairman, Tata Group 1990-2004)

Decision making is an inevitable part of any business. In fact, as one of my professors told me many years ago, **"Never be in doubt. Even when you don't take a decision, you are making a decision."** The fact of the matter is that there is no escaping for either an entrepreneur or business leader from the decision-making process. At the most, it is possible only to delay the making of the decision. However, no individual or organisation can avoid decision making permanently. As I like to put it, **"Such is the reality of the world around us: if you do not make the decision, the decision will be made for you."**

As an entrepreneur, you must look to decision making as an integral and fundamental part of business, so fundamental, in fact, that the success or failure of your business depends on it. It is important to remember that whether a decision is right or wrong will only be revealed after the decision is taken and that too happens after a considerable passage of time. However, that should not be the reason why you should evade or prevent yourself from taking them. In fact, the success of any business leader or organisation lies within their decision-making process. Being successful in any field requires simply that the percentages of correct decisions taken must always be higher than the percentages of wrong decisions taken. Believe me when I tell you this: It's as simple as that.

Tata Nano – The Car that Should Not Exist

It was in the year 2002 that Ratan Tata, the chairman of one of India's oldest and most respected conglomerates, witnessed the near-fatal accident of a family on a scooter in Bangalore. This incident had such a profound effect on him that it made him put in place plans to produce a reasonably priced and super safe car for the common man. It is important to mention here that the Tata Group was not a stranger to the automobile industry. They were already one of the oldest producers of heavy transport vehicles in India. Furthermore, under the stewardship of Ratan Tata, it was already in the passenger car business with the introduction of the Tata Sumo (1994) and Indica (1998).

In the initial stages of developing the Nano, the aim was to create a compact sedan which was both functional and affordable for the Indian family. In fact, it was only when a reporter with a British newspaper questioned Ratan Tata about the possible price of such a car at the Geneva Motor Show did he quote the figure Rs. 100,000 or $2,000. This one statement became the headline in the next edition of the newspaper, and so, in this way, it was broadcasted to the world that the Tata Group was about to produce the world's cheapest family car.

A family car for just Rs. 100,000 or $2,000 was an unheard concept in the automotive world. The task was daunting, to say the least, but in the mind of Ratan Tata, it was not an impossible one. He immediately set about achieving his goal. Ratan Tata gave three essential requirements to his chosen team leader, Girish Wagh; they were as follows: First, it should be low cost to manufacture. Secondly, it must adhere to all regulatory and mandatory rules and regulations within the state of India. Third and finally, it should be fuel-efficient, and at the same time, in no way should the overall performance of the vehicle be compromised.

Girish Wagh was in no doubt of the intimidating task which had been assigned to him. He was quick to realise that the entire project would require him to create a revolutionary new manufacturing process. The design of the vehicle itself was a major challenge. To counter the increase in cost, the engineers at the Tata Group introduced a new and small designed engine placed under the rear seat of the vehicle. The team introduced similar mechanisms for the right and left side of the door. The instrument cluster was placed in the middle of the dashboard so that it could be utilised for both left and right-hand drive vehicles. Once the design was complete, then came the daunting task of manufacturing the vehicle itself. To this effect, he went about creating a completely new distribution process. He introduced the concept of involving new entrepreneurs and vendors who might want to establish manufacturing facilities of their own, i.e. he wished to outsource the manufacturing of certain parts of the vehicle, which would, in turn, lead to cost-saving at the point of manufacturing. Thus, it was imperative to evolve a system which would facilitate seamless interaction between the design team and manufacturing team. However, the number of personnel in both teams was constantly increasing. In fact, the number of personnel, consisting of entrepreneurs, vendors, designer and engineers, had reached a mammoth figure of over 500.

Yet, Wagh was up to that challenge as well. He formed teams within the personnel involved and delegated powers and appointed leaders. He re-engineered his daily routine in such a way that every morning he spent around two hours on the factory floor so as to filter through feedback and accelerate the decision-making process. He further reported his progress to Ratan Tata, who would himself visit the Pune factory for regular updates. After numerous ups and downs and several setbacks and improvements, Ratan Tata launched Tata Nano at a glittering function in Mumbai on January 10, 2008.

Since its introduction, the Tata Nano has sold over 130,000 (2008-2015) units. It is still the world's cheapest car in production. It is also a matter of pride that the development of the car has led to 31 design and 37 technology patents being filed. Thus, there is no doubt that Ratan Tata delivered on his promise in realising his dream as well as fulfilled the aspirations of millions of Indian families to become first-time car owners. One of his competitors remarked after the launch of the Tata Nano, **"Next time Ratan Tata has an idea, don't tell him it can't be done."**

Through the Tata Nano story, I would like to draw your attention to **three critical areas** with regard to decision making. The first and perhaps the most important is the decision-making style utilised by the top rung leadership of an organisation. The second is the decision-making process employed throughout the organisation to fulfil the decision of the top rung leaders. And finally, the many other factors which can have the ability to influence or should be considered at the time of making the final decision.

Decision-Making Styles

In theory, there are four main styles of decision making. They are known as the directive, analytic, conceptual and behavioural styles. That being said, it is rare to find a decision-maker who fits completely in only one style. In fact, in most cases, the decision-maker is a combination of more than one style. In my opinion, it is the circumstances or events that allow a good decision-maker to seamlessly move around all the different styles of decision making. To put it candidly, decision-makers must be able to adapt their decision-making style to the situation at hand. Each style processes information differently; thus, it should come as no surprise that the final decision which results is a sum total of the style employed and is unique and particular to the characteristics of the individual applying it.

Directive Style

The directive style of decision making is usually employed when there is a need for quick results. It is an aggressive style where the decision-maker will rely on his own information and experience. Should he or she be leading a team, then the decision-maker will expect the members of his team to carry out his instructions without question. The characteristics of a directive style leader are that they are rational and have a low tolerance for ambiguity. They are strict in following the rules and are excellent communicators. On the negative side, they are prone to making silly mistakes as, most often, they are required to make quick decisions with limited amounts of information. Furthermore, they are seen to be reluctant to approach others for opinions and suggestions.

The directive style approach is best suited to short-term results but not for long-term solutions.

Analytic Style

The analytical style of decision making is usually employed when there is sufficient time available for a decision to be made. This style of decision making is very slow and time-consuming. The analytical decision-maker takes time to review all the information at hand. In fact, they are diligent as well as meticulous and analyse all aspects of a problem before coming up with the final decision. This leads them to be overly cautious and controlling over all aspects of the decision-making process. The advantage of employing such a decision-making style is that it allows one to have the ability to adapt and cope with unique situations as and when they arise. However, it invariably leads to the final decision being delayed and thus, in turn, leads to loss of time, effort and financial resources.

Conceptual Style

The conceptual style of decision making is best described as a creative and artistic style of looking at a problem. Conceptual decision-makers are achievement-oriented and focus on the long-term effects of a decision. It is this focus on the long term which allows them to be very good at finding suitable solutions. They are regularly found to suggest out of the box ideas, which they acquire through a detailed approach to the problem at hand. In almost all cases, their decisions are based on a broad outlook of the situation at hand, and their solutions to these problems are intuitive, futuristic and path-breaking in nature.

Behavioural Style

The behavioural style of decision making is best described as a consensus-built decision. Behavioural decision-makers are masters at convincing and persuasion. They are most effective where there is a need for building agreement within a group. They look at many alternative solutions to a problem and then look at ways to convince the other group members towards that solution. This type of decision-makers work around the negatives and reconcile the differences within a group. The end result is that the whole group feels that they have participated and contributed to the ultimate solution to the problem at hand. This, in turn, leads to the growth of unity and trust within all the members of the decision-making group.

Conclusion

In conclusion, while it is absolutely true that a majority of entrepreneurs and business leaders will have a dominant style when it comes to making decisions, the best or the most sought-after leaders are those who have an inherent ability to adapt and transform their style based on the need of the situation. In the majority of situations, they prefer to build consensus within their group before arriving at a final decision. Nevertheless, it is pertinent to point out here that in all cases, it is the entrepreneur and leader who will ultimately be held responsible for the final outcome of that decision.

The Decision-Making Process

A good decision is rarely impulsive. Good decisions are an outcome of a well-structured decision-making process. While in theory there may be a number of steps which can be involved in arriving at a final decision, in real life, the decision-making process can be filtered down to five simple steps. These steps are the following:

Understand the Problem

The first step in the decision-making process is to understand the problem. It is the duty of every leader and entrepreneur to master the ability to define a problem. Understanding a problem means to discover all the layers which have led to the creation of the said problem. There is always a core issue to a problem, which may or may not be evident at the very beginning. It is also true that should this core issue not be discovered, the problem will continue to persist. Therefore, it is essential to spend time to understand all the aspects of the problem in its entirety before even beginning to look for a resolution to the problem. As **Albert Einstein** once remarked, **"If I were given one hour to save the planet, I would spend 59 minutes defining the problem and one minute resolving it."**

Share the Problem

One of the surest ways of solving a problem in any organisational setup is to allow an open dialogue on the problem. It is prudent to seek the opinions of people that you trust in the way of mentors, experts and professionals. More essentially, all stakeholders should be encouraged to share their insight when a problem arises. This sharing of information further allows the leader or entrepreneur to tap into the vast reservoir of real-time life experience of all the stakeholders. This, in turn, allows for many alternative solutions to be suggested for the same problem. Sharing the problem, in essence, allows a vital understanding of the various factors directly related to the problem. It is always a good practice to gather as many resources as possible in order to make the best decision.

Synthesise All the Alternatives

At this stage in the decision-making process, each decision-maker would have already decided on the criteria on which they would base the final solution to the problem. He or she would now spend time in carefully sorting and evaluating all the possible solutions to the problem. In fact, it is an essential prerequisite to clearly understand the various pros and cons of each of the alternative solutions. In almost all cases, the final solution will be a combination of the alternative solutions which are best suited to the predetermined criteria of the decision-maker. In essence, it is important to realise that the leader or entrepreneur will find a solution which is able to gain the most benefit for the organisation in the long term.

Take the Decision and Implement It

This step is the most important one of all. Many decision-makers are found to be nervous or unsure at this stage of the decision-making process. However, it is essential to remember that there is no turning back from making a final decision. Once the decision is made, there is nothing else to do but implement the decision. In actual fact, **a decision has no value unless you put it into action.**

Review the Decision (After Some Time)

In practice, it is not always possible for any decision-maker to prepare for all the contingencies that the ultimate decision may have on the future of the organisation. It is sometimes deemed necessary to make certain changes in the decision, to adapt to the changes in the organisation's operating environment both internal and external, in order to yield the maximum benefit for the organisation as a whole.

Factors that Affect Decision Making

Change is an inevitable part of the business environment. With the passage of time, various factors begin to influence the decision-making process of an organisation. These factors may be both internal and external in nature. What is important to realise is that those organisations which are either slow or refuse to adapt themselves to the changes in the business environment are doomed to fail. Some internal and external factors are briefly discussed below:

Internal Factors

Internal factors simply mean those factors which affect the organisation from within. Some internal factors are as follows:

Change in Leadership

A change in the leadership of an organisation has a direct effect on the decision-making process. A leadership change influences the thinking process and the working method of an organisation. It is an inevitable fact that the new leadership will introduce new practices within the organisation. A new leader at any level can single-handedly influence the very direction of a company. This change at the very top of the organisation in almost all cases is percolated downwards to all levels of management. Therefore, any change, whether that is at the board level or at management level, should be well investigated and all its possible aspects should be fully explored before any change is finally implemented within an organisation.

Illustration

The appointment of J.R.D. Tata as chairman of the Tata Group, who is credited for diversifying the business group in various industries such as tea (Tata Tea), air-conditioning and allied products (Voltas) and even watches (Titan Industries). What is also most impressive about the leadership of Jehangir Ratanji Dadabhoy (J.R.D.) Tata was that when he took over the stewardship of the Tata Group in 1935, the group was involved in 14 different enterprises. At the time of his retirement in 1988, the Tata Group held the controlling interest in over 95 different enterprises throughout the world.

Production Capacity

The proper utilisation of production capacity directly affects the revenues generated by an organisation. Any firm, whether a manufacturer or a service provider, must focus its efforts on achieving the optimal use of its production capacity. For this reason alone, almost all successful organisations formulate a strategy to produce goods and services in a cost-effective manner. In simple terms, optimum production capacity is achieved when production capabilities meet demand. Optimum utilisation of production leads to cost benefits. These benefits directly translate to saving and an increase in the profit margin of an organisation.

Illustration

Bajaj Auto in the 1970s. In this period, there existed a licence raj in India which restricted the production capacity of various commercial products. Bajaj Auto was able to produce more scooters than their permissible quota, as they continuously focused on improving and reducing the production time of their scooters. An interesting fact is that, though there were many competitors in the market, the Bajaj Auto scooter, even with a waiting period of over 10 years, was by far the most popular scooter in India during that time. In fact, the Bajaj Auto two-wheeler is regarded by many as one of the biggest success stories of the Indian automotive industry.

Quality of Human Resources

The quality of human resources is a very important factor which affects the decision-making process within an organisation. It may seem to the untrained eye that it is the top rung management or leadership which is responsible for the success of the organisation. However, the real people who are responsible for the success of any successful organisation are, in fact, the different and unique individuals who work at different levels within that organisation. One of the most basic truths in any business is that the success of an organisation depends on the people who work within it. It is the different and unique skills and abilities of these people which are always ultimately responsible for the success or failure of an organisation.

Illustration

The appointment of Mr Nandan Nilekani in 2009 as the chairman of the Unique Identification Authority of India (UIDAI), tasked with the responsibility to create and implement the Aadhaar card. The objective of the Aadhar card was to create a Multipurpose National Identity Card which would help in the distribution of various welfare benefits to the citizens of India. Mr Nandan Nilekani was handpicked by Mr Manmohan Singh, the then prime minister of India, and accorded the status of a cabinet minister in the Government of India. At the time of its implementation, this unique system was regarded as the largest social project on the planet. On 29th November 2010, Ranjana Sonawane became India's first Unique ID card holder. And on 26th November 2012, the first transfer of welfare benefits took place through the scheme. Till the year 2015-2016, a total of Rs. 5981 crore or US$890 million was spent on the implementation of this National Identity scheme.

External Factors

Those factors which have the potential to influence and affect the decision-making process of an organisation, and thus have a direct influence of its performance from the outside, are regarded as external factors. Some of these external factors are discussed below:

Enactment of Laws

All organisations are subject to the laws, rules and regulation of the environment they operate within. These rules often vary because of the location and position of the organisation around the world. An organisation is governed first by the laws of the country and the state in which they operate and, in addition, are also subject to local and municipal rules and regulations. To this effect, they are subject to various types of taxes, liabilities and official fees. In normal practice, all these expenses play an integral part in determining the financial position of the organisation. Any change in the law can have both an adverse as well as positive influence on an organisation.

Illustration

The demonetisation of Rs. 1000 and Rs. 500 notes in India on the 8th of November 2016. As of that date, all notes of the above denomination ceased to be legal tender throughout India. The effect of this law was that all individuals and business organisations would have to deposit the now-defunct currency and exchange the same for newly designed notes. This demonetisation is regarded as India's most potent strike on hoarding of unaccounted money in the last three decades. This one change of law has affected all the different strata throughout the general population of India. The effect of the enactment of this law has forced both individuals and business organisations to review their decision-making process. It is estimated that the change of this law will affect the way of conducting business in India for many years to come.

Technological Change

The effect of technology has a direct impact on the structure and flow of work within an organisation. A prime example of such change is seen in the rapid automation of workspaces (**computerisation and electronic networking**) at different levels within an organisation. Advancement of technology has the unique distinction of both creating and eliminating job roles and designations within all spheres of a business establishment. It is estimated that there will continue to be rapid advancement of technologies both within and outside the business environment. These improvements will, in turn, force organisations to adopt these new technologies within their already established working environment. Thus, with each addition or redundancy of technology within an organisation, the decision-making process will be affected to a great degree. In fact, there is little doubt that those organisations and establishments who respond the most rapidly to this technology change will be most benefited in the long run.

Illustration

Kodak and its underestimation of the digital revolution. In a study conducted by Harvard University in the year 1976, it was found that the Kodak Company had a virtual monopoly over the camera and camera film industry around the world. Kodak singularly accounted for over 85% of camera sales and over 90% of camera film sales in the United States alone. The company had a strategy of selling its cameras at a cheaper price but regularly increased the price of its camera film, thus maintaining an ever-rising profit margin.

Over a period of time, technology changed and the world welcomed the digital revolution. This was most evident with the introduction of cameras in cell phones and the convenience of digital storage provided in the mobile instrument itself. Over the next few years, both the camera and camera film business were made obsolete. To put it bluntly, the management of the Kodak Company was unable to appropriately gauge the effects of digitalisation on their business environment. These miscalculations led them to react slowly and resulted in the overall failure of the organisation as a whole. This can be assessed from the fact that while the company employed 145,000 people worldwide in the year 1988, most recently, the Kodak Company accounts for only around 18,000 employees.

External Competition

Many experts regard the most critical business factor to be external competition. For all entrepreneurs and leaders, it is important to both recognise and understand the competitive landscape in which their organisations operate. It is imperative to conduct a competitive analysis study so as to adequately compare the products and services offered by competing organisations. The direct result of such a study is to create business policies which, in turn, lead to quality products and enhance customer services and satisfaction. Competition ultimately guarantees operational efficiency, which then helps an organisation build competitive advantages that derive benefit for the organisation in the long term. A harsh truth in the business environment is that organisations who fail to keep pace with their competitors will eventually be overwhelmed and, as often is the case, will be doomed to fail.

Illustration

The global cola wars between Coca Cola and Pepsi is a prime example of this. When Coca Cola returned to India in the year 1997, it quickly became aware of the dominant position of Pepsi in the Indian market. Pepsi focused on advertisements which featured cricketers and film stars, which were immensely popular and widely accepted within the Indian society as a whole. On the other hand, Coca Cola followed their global strategy of dependence on attractive jingles and advertisements which were centred on Indian culture and society. Coca Cola soon realised that their campaign was failing miserably for the most part because of their campaign's inability to link up and connect with the general Indian population.

In fact, things came to the forefront when Coca Cola successfully bid to become the official sponsor of the 1997 Cricket World Cup. Pepsi countered with one of the most brilliant campaigns on record till date with the **'Nothing Official About It'** campaign. The end result was that even though Coca Cola was the official sponsor, it was the Pepsi advertisements which were able to influence the hearts and minds of the general Indian public. However, Coca Cola also had its revenge when it was able to successfully outbid Pepsi for the television rights of the Pepsi Asia Cup held in the same year, almost immediately after the Cricket World Cup of 1997. This was not the only incident between the two global beverage giants. Both Coca Cola and Pepsi still continue to spend millions of dollars throughout the world in their attempt to become the global leader of the cola beverage industry.

In conclusion, the business environment is a sum total of all the internal and external factors which from time to time exert their pressure on an organisation. All successful leaders and entrepreneurs, without exception, focus their energies on recognising these factors and then innovate and advance practical ideas to protect their institution against any malevolent effect.

Chapter Six

The Gentle Art of Saying No... No! No!

"The art of leadership is saying no, not saying yes.
It is very easy to say yes."

Tony Blair
(Prime Minister, United Kingdom (1997-2007))

People, on the whole, do not react well when their ideas or proposals are turned down. However, if a business is to be successful, the management will have to get comfortable with using the 'no' word quite frequently and without any hesitation or doubt. This being said, successful entrepreneurs and leaders know the art of saying no. This art is perhaps one of the most difficult to master, yet it is an attribute which one must adopt if one is to achieve success in their enterprise or organisation.

Entrepreneurs and leaders are presented with new proposals, opportunities and partnerships almost on a daily basis. They are well aware that refusing such proposals or ideas will lead them to be not only unpopular but also disliked by a few individuals or a small group within their organisation. However, they do so in order to keep themselves and their organisation on track to the aims and objectives for which the organisation has been actually created or formed.

By saying no, they are setting up their boundaries while at the same time maintaining their relationship with their employees and colleagues. Most definitely, this is not easy to do, but when saying no is done with care and respect, the act of saying no is beneficial to both the parties concerned. Therefore, it is highly recommended and often practised to put in place a well-planned and professional method of saying no to both people and their proposals.

Through this chapter, I wish you to realise **why** it is important to say no. And most importantly, what the possible techniques are which can be utilised in mastering the **gentle art of saying no.**

The Why???

Saying No Saves Time

Such is the nature of things that we have only 24 hours in a day. Therefore, it is important to have control over this time. To control this time, it is imperative that it be allocated properly. In fact, all leaders and entrepreneurs are extremely selfish with their time. They try and prioritise their schedules months in advance. They set their timetable as they want as per their needs and requirements. They rarely will allow any other person to determine how they spend their precious time. The rationale behind this habit is simple: whenever you decide to allocate your time to the objectives and goals of another person or organisation, you are giving away a valuable and costly commodity. The time you have should be utilised in achieving your own objectives and goals.

Therefore, realise that time is a rare and valuable commodity. It is a limited resource due to its availability being measured in days, months and years. We do not even know how much each person is allocated in one lifetime. As a result, we are duty-bound to decide how, when and where our time is utilised so that it best serves our needs and our requirements.

More Energy

Take a good look at any of the top business leaders and entrepreneurs throughout the world. They always seem to be bursting with extra energy. They always come across as glowing with passion, and invariably, they are able to transfer some of their energy to the people they meet. These leaders have discovered a new-age mantra. That new-age mantra is **'Manage your energy, rather than your time'**. In simple terms, an effective leader or entrepreneur is able to identify the critical areas of their business which require their immediate attention. Once these areas are identified, they then plan how to save their energy so as to give those critical areas their paramount and undivided attention.

The core reason for doing this is that focusing on the really important problems first will allow the other members in their team to focus on the other less important issues so that, in tandem, the entire team resolves the issue at hand and all members of the team save their energy. In short, by not allowing each other's energy to be wasted on repetitive and routine work, the job at hand is resolved in a much shorter time, resulting in a saving of time for all individuals. This, in turn, may be utilised in resolving other issues in another area of the business.

Saying No Forces the Creation of Alternatives

Many times, successful leaders and entrepreneurs arbitrarily reject a proposal or solution outright. While to the untrained eye this convention may seem unfair and demeaning in nature, one of the primary reasons this is done is to force the individual or the team to come up with a better-researched proposal or a better-enhanced solution. It percolates from the belief that every problem must have alternative solutions. Furthermore, the best solution will either come in the form of an alternative solution or will be a combination of various alternative solutions.

A few other reasons why successful leaders and entrepreneurs arbitrarily say no is to gain more time to reach a final decision or, in some cases, to encourage the members of an organisation to realise the correct solution on their own. The fact of the matter is that once they respond in the affirmative to any proposal or solution, they can rarely be seen as retreating from their commitment and obligation.

Your Yes is Valued More

It is ironic, but true, that when you learn to say no, your yes becomes more valuable. The people around you realise that you cannot be taken for granted. Furthermore, your subordinates and team members recognise that they will have to work hard for your final approval. One of the most evident changes will be that anyone coming to you for your approval will spend considerable time working on the proposals they will make to you. In simple terms, your yes to their proposal will become a stamp of approval which will further enhance their confidence at the workplace. On the personal front, the persons in your team will realise your importance in the decision-making process of the organisation. They will realise that your saying no is ultimately for the larger benefit of the organisation. This realisation will lead them to respect you for your decisions.

The Gentle Art of Saying No

Check Your Tone

This is one of the most important rules which must be followed while using the word 'no'. A great deal of ill-feeling and bitterness can be avoided by keeping our voice at a respectable level while refusing a proposal. Keeping our tone in check allows us to project a sense of respect as well as authority at the same time. Therefore, it a highly appreciated attribute to possess when dealing with people in different strata of the organisation. In simple terms, there is no reason to be rude or offensive to an individual while saying no to them. Therefore, keeping our tone in check is an essential necessity which directly relates to the success of an organisation.

Tell Them Why

A key strategy which is employed while saying no is explaining why the no is being said in the first place. In business as well as other areas of life, preserving a relationship is essential. It is important to draw on personal experience. How many times have we all just been told no, without any reason or justification? Therefore, is it not fair to assume that others also deserve a fair answer to their rejection? All successful entrepreneurs and leaders take time to explain the rationale of their refusal to the concerned individual or group. They share very judicially the reasons for their decision and even offer alternative suggestions on how the proposal may be improved so as to be approved at a later date.

Take Some Time Before Giving a Final Reply

An essential attribute of successful entrepreneurs and leaders is that they rarely refuse a suggestion or proposal without taking time to think it over in its entirety. They are consistent in buying time before coming up with their final no. This practice of taking time helps them not only to evaluate all the pros and cons of the proposal but also helps them to come up with a substantial reason for denying the proposal. In almost all cases, they spend this time to look into their other commitments and priorities. This further allows them to determine if they can spare their time and resources on the new proposal. Therefore, it is seen that once a decision is reached to refuse a proposal, they share that decision immediately. The objective is to make clear that this decision of refusal has come after careful consideration.

Managing the Ego

Sometimes a difficult situation arises in an organisation when an important and influential member of the team comes up with a proposal. The situation becomes difficult as it places the entrepreneur or leader in a situation where it becomes complicated to know how he or she would go about refusing such a proposal. In these cases, the situation can be diffused commonly by using the term **'It's not you, it's me'.** Such situations are learning points in an organisation. They can be solved by re-enforcing to the proposer that their proposal or idea is a good one and the decision-making body appreciates the time and effort the individual or the team has put into the proposal. However, sometimes even the best proposals cannot be approved. The entrepreneur or leader shows him or herself to be the weak link within the organisation and shows he or she is the reason for the proposal being rejected. In this way, he or she assumes all the responsibility of the rejection, at the same time satisfying the individual or the team that though the proposal is rejected for now, it may be taken up at a future date.

Silence Means No!

Remaining silent is also one of the most effective ways of saying no. Sometimes a situation may arise where certain individuals are unable to accept the rejection of their proposal. To this effect, they will continuously persist in presenting the same proposal time and time again. In cases such as this, every effort should be made to explain to them the causes of this rejection. Should these individuals continue to persist even after some time, it is best that they are left alone. This can be done by remaining absolutely silent when they raise the proposal again. This silence should hopefully make them aware that there is no chance of reconsideration of your judgement and your decision is full and final.

Accept that You Might Have to Say Yes

It cannot be denied that the business landscape is in fluid form and is constantly changing. A proposal which may have been rejected in the past suddenly may become the most significant and crucial scheme to the growth of the business. To this effect, successful entrepreneurs and leaders are never afraid of re-visiting any proposal from the past. In fact, in most cases, they are found to regularly keep an eye on the new developments within their business industry. As and when the opportunity arises, they themselves will re-activate the proposal so to gain the most benefit for themselves and their organisation.

In the end, entrepreneurs and business leaders are well aware that a business requires absolute focus and dedication to be made into a success. Setting limits is essentially not only good for the health of their businesses but also for their peace of mind. So, without a doubt, one of the more important habits or practices to adopt is to get comfortable with using the 'no' word. That being said, saying no is difficult, but finding a way to reach goals and objectives together is an accurate measure of true leadership. The next time you need to turn down a request or proposal, use the above-presented approach to let someone down gently.

The ABCD Method of Saying No!

I could not bring myself to end this chapter before introducing you to perhaps the most original method of saying no. This technique is utilised in almost all private, semi-private and governmental organisations throughout India. In fact, even our current prime minister, Narendra Modi, referred to its existence when he was addressing a meeting in 2014, when he said, **"There was a need to transform from the culture of Avoid, Bypass, Confuse, Delay to a culture of Responsibility, Ownership, Accountability, Discipline." (Business Standard,** December 29, 2014 **)**

A = Avoid

This method of saying no is usually employed by individuals who have the power to make a decision but are averse to doing so. To this effect, this type of decision-makers tries their best to keep away from being drawn into the decision-making process. These individuals are always busy with some other work or are out for meetings. In fact, they have perfected the art of attending office but are always found missing when duty calls. Therefore, in simple terms, they spend their time finding ways to avoid doing any work. However, when they are unable to avoid the work at hand even by their best efforts, they then proceed to try and bypass it.

B = Bypass

The second method of avoiding work is to bypass it. The core of this method is to get another individual of the same designation to do the work for you. That is to say, all the files and paper trails of the job will mysteriously appear on the desk of another individual. At times, simple avoidance could fail to work. Then the second logical avoidance mechanism comes into play: bypass the decision. Puzzling definitions and language in the delegation of authority and discretionary powers come to the rescue. There is also a refusal to understand the nuances of a foreign language that happens to be India's official language. Thus, the bosses will refuse to accept a simple sentence like, "In view of a growth in sales of 25% and of 45% in profitability, the performance of the venture is considered satisfactory". Some of them would insist that the word "considered" be removed from the quoted sentence in board memorandum. Sometimes excuses will be found by passing the decision making to a subordinate or to a superior.

The basic idea is simple. If you cannot avoid it, then try to bypass it.

C = Confuse

When avoidance and bypassing have failed and the file with its bulky collection of correspondence is back on your table, then comes the time for creativity. Look for the real issue and confuse it. It often takes the shape of forming a committee to study related issues and make recommendations. In the present scenario of the forthcoming Lok Sabha election, it could have been calling for an all-party meet and forming a committee of leaders taken from all parties to list merits and demerits of all candidates while recommending a panel of three candidates. Or in the context of common entrance test for engineering/ medical colleges, forming a committee of members from each state's education board, university and academic institution granted autonomy so generously in the last two decades.

D = Do

By the time you are through with the three stages of postponement and avoidance, the chances are that a situation would have been raised that forces someone else to take an ultimate decision. Or there may suddenly arise a situation which renders the entire decision making a futile exercise. But due to your fortune or since the almighty has been kind, the matter has come back resolved to you after going round in circles for an intolerable length of time and then you might as well do it.

Now that you have become aware of the ABCD Principle of Management universally followed by some administrators in private, semi-private and governmental organisations, you would surely find their behaviour and attitude a bit less frustrating than before.

Chapter Seven

Communication... Communication... Communication

"Communication is the key for any global business."

Anita Roddick
(Founder, The Body Shop)

"You can have brilliant ideas, but if you can't get them across, Your ideas won't get you anywhere."

Lee Iacocca
(President, CEO, Chairman – Chrysler 1978-1992)

Good communication skills are essential in a business environment. It is this skill which allows an individual the ability to effectively communicate with people in a wide variety of situations. Simply put, in today's age of globalisation, an entrepreneur and leader will need to communicate with people not only from different countries but also with people of different age groups, cultures, orientations and different levels of experience. These leaders are well aware that only correctly communicating their thoughts and ideas will lead to the development of their business. After all, it cannot be denied that the way a top leader or entrepreneur communicates is a direct reflection on the image and reputation of any organisation.

It is a widely accepted fact that only 15% of all business communication is formal in nature. Furthermore, the majority of that communication is in the form of verbal or written communication. In essence, it is these forms of communication which are for the most part responsible for the success or failure of any business organisation. Through this chapter, I wish to highlight the importance of effective communication within a business organisation as well as introduce certain techniques by which both verbal and written communication can be effectively improved within any and all establishments.

Benefits of Effective Communication

To be a success in any business, it is imperative to understand why effective communication within an organisation is so important. While it is easy to say that good communication is beneficial within an organisation, the most successful entrepreneurs and leaders focus to create a workforce which has the ability to communicate not only within the confines of the workplace but, more importantly, also communicate with their customers, vendors and business partners.

Smooth Flow of Instructions

A business organisation is set up to achieve certain goals and objectives. All organisations, big or small, have a well-defined hierarchy. In simple terms, the top management decides what the objectives are and, more importantly, which methods are to be employed to achieve the desired results. The success of any organisation will depend on how clearly the top management is able to transmit these objectives and methods throughout the entire organisational setup. Therefore, it is regularly observed that successful organisations focus a lot of time and energy on constantly upgrading their internal communication channels so as to make them more transparent, free-flowing and result-oriented.

Ideas and Innovations

Once the goals and objectives have been decided by the top management of an organisation, they are further divided into smaller targets and transmitted down throughout the organisation. The job of achieving these targets becomes the duty of the employees. As mentioned earlier, in most cases, the top management generally also defines a method on how the targets are to be achieved. However, the business environment of any organisation is in a constant flow of change. Therefore, there is a constant need to adapt the predefined method to achieve the desired result. In organisations where the management is proactive in seeking the ideas and feedback of their employees and subordinates, the employees will also respond with new and better suggestions. This, in turn, leads to more innovative and enhanced products and services, thereby giving the organisation an opportunity to augment their profits and become even more successful.

Enhances Teamwork

Effective communication within an organisation allows for the formation of highly dedicated and efficient teams. In almost all cases, effective communication provides employees both with knowledge and support through a well-placed structure. More importantly, it provides a comfortable and safe environment to resolve complex situations and issues effectively. Effective communication leads to the growth of trust and loyalty within almost all individuals and departments within an organisation. The end result is the formation of a cohesive unit dedicated to achieving the goals and objectives of the organisation. Furthermore, when there is free communication within all levels of hierarchy, it fosters positive relationships and bonding that benefit the organisation as a whole.

Employees Promote the Organisation

Effective communication helps establish a healthy dialogue between employee and employer. The more the employees are aware of what is expected from them, the easier it becomes for them to be more productive at their job. In most cases, other than just the financial stability, employees also seek respect and appreciation for the work they do in the organisation. There is no better publicity than a satisfied employee. In fact, when employees actively promote the services of their own organisation within their community, it enhances the reputation of the organisation and further promotes the business, which then leads to higher profits and is highly beneficial to the organisation in the long term.

Growth Through Diversity

In today's day and age, organisations throughout the world are actively seeking newer pastures for their growth. To this effect, they are intensely focusing on growth by setting up subsidiaries and partnerships in different parts of the world. It is, therefore, a common situation to find them dealing with both language and cultural differences on a regular basis. Organisations have, therefore, begun to actively invest in educating their employees to communicate effectively with their international counterparts. It is also true that these subsidiaries and partnerships bring with them better operational and functional strategies which enhance and improve the core competencies of the organisation as a whole. When these newer approaches are effectively communicated through the hierarchy system, it enhances the global competitiveness of the original organisation. The end result is that the organisation becomes a learning organisation such that it is able to improve itself and gain further beneficial advantages beyond its domestic borders.

Verbal Communication

In its simplest definition, when information is shared between an individual or group by the use of speech, it is known as verbal communication. It includes one-syllable sounds as well as complex discussions and depends heavily not only on language but also on tone and emotion. The ultimate objective of verbal communication is that it communicates the same thought between the participants and produces the desired effect or reaction.

When the same individuals interact in a business environment, verbal communication serves as a medium to express ideas and concepts which are vital for the internal and external growth of a business organisation. Verbal communication within an organisation encompasses various individuals and groups in varied strata all consistently working towards a common goal and objective. These will include not only co-workers, subordinates, employees but also clients and customers. It is also true that the very nature of verbal communication goes through a substantial evolution as it occurs in various other contexts such as group discussions, training sessions, interviews, consultations, performance appraisals and so on and so forth. To this effect, an entrepreneur or business leader must possess the ability to convey information both clearly and effectively throughout his organisation. It should, therefore, come as no surprise that these business leaders also look to hire those employees who are able to understand this information as well as utilise it in the correct manner and, more importantly, are able to communicate it as it was originally intended.

Illustration: Immediately... Without Delay

The Berlin wall, also referred to as the iron curtain, physically divided the city of Berlin, leading to the creation of East and West Germany from 1961 to 1989. The construction of the wall led to severe travel restrictions between the two Germanys. The restriction was so severe that for a border which spanned over 140 kilometres, there were only nine points for entry and exit. Furthermore, as time progressed, there was a revival in the demand to unify the two Germanys into a single, consolidated country. The people of East Germany, who were most affected by these restrictions, were able to apply some pressure so as to force a change in these restrictive measures.

On November 9th, 1989, the East German government finally relented and passed a new regulation which was aimed at facilitating easy travel between the two German sides. Once passed, the duty of announcing the new measures fell on the shoulders of Gunter Schabowski. He was an East German official who regularly briefed the press and world media on official events within East Germany. On that day, when he was handed the speech he was meant to deliver, he assumed it contained an insignificant announcement; he did not even read it before he advanced to the podium.

Gunter Schabowski casually remarked that the East German government had decided to lift the travel restrictions across its border with West Germany. When pressed by the reporters as to when this restriction would be lifted, he fumbled over his papers and nervously responded of his own accord, **"Immediately... Without delay"**. This one statement lead to a cascading effect: On one side, the reporters present broadcasted to the world the wrong information that the Berlin wall was coming down that night itself, which, in turn, caused large masses of people to congregate on both sides of the wall in anticipation of the unification of Germany.

The rest, as we know, is history. Despite the fact that there was a large contingent of guards posted at the wall, given the sheer number of people, they had no option but to step back. Sometime later, the people themselves started to break through the wall. Thus, only due to the wrong verbal communication of an ill-prepared government official, the whole of Germany was reunited after 28 long years.

The above illustration shows the need for proper and effective verbal communication in all organisational setups. It points out in no uncertain terms that if the correct message is not transmitted all the way down the hierarchy, it can lead to disastrous events.

Let us now look at what the techniques are by which effective verbal communication within an organisation can be improved.

Techniques to Improve Verbal Communication

As presented earlier, there are many measurable benefits to be gained from communicating effectively within an organisation. However, it is also true that all employees will not have the same level of proficiency when it comes to this skill set. This being said, it is always possible to educate and improve an individual's ability to verbally communicate effectively. Some techniques for doing this are shared below:

Do Your Homework

In any organisation, meetings are both essential and a necessity. They are by far the most preferred method to encourage interaction between employees, clients and other individuals. And there is little doubt about the advantages it brings in regard to problem-solving of any kind or of any magnitude. It is of primary importance that those participating in any interaction be able to communicate their point of view to all persons present. Furthermore, they must have facts and figures to defend their position. Therefore, it is highly recommended that all individuals in any business meeting spend some time to predict and prepare for any difficult situations which may arise during such interactions.

Be Concise

All verbal communications in any business interaction must be time-bound. All participants involved in the interaction must be encouraged to put their point across in a concise and well-structured manner. Being concise is the characteristic of a well-prepared and well-informed mind. In fact, many entrepreneurs and business leaders appreciate individuals who are able to present to them the correct picture of any situation in the shortest period of time, thus allowing them the advantage of making the correct decision and allowing them the ability to allocate the remaining time to other important areas of the business.

Speak Slowly

Speaking slowly is by far one of the most overlooked attributes with regard to effective verbal communication. Speaking slowly allows for two major advantages when verbally communicating with other individuals. First, it allows you to be heard word for word, so your message is communicated well. The second and most important advantage is that it allows our thoughts to stay in sync with our words, so it acts as a barrier from saying something we do not want or do not mean to communicate.

Tailor Conversation to Your Audience

In a business environment, we verbally communicate with various individuals both internal and external to the organisation. Therefore, it is essential for a person to be flexible in his communication skill when dealing with the different branches of the organisational structure. There is a marked difference when communicating with a co-worker or supplier vis-a-vis communicating with a senior or a customer. Each interaction is in essence very diverse from the other. Therefore, it is important to tailor-make our communication to the required level as and when it is needed so that it leads to the message being communicated as effectively as possible.

Improve Your Vocabulary

One of the prerequisites of any interaction is the use of appropriate and relevant words. The use of correct words within verbal communication plays an important part in its effective understanding. Therefore, learning new words and using them at the appropriate time will allow an individual to relate to the interaction in a much more positive and constructive way. It also allows for self-development, which is always beneficial to the organisation in the long run.

Watch Your Body Language

It is important to remember that while verbally interacting in a group, we also send out some non-verbal communications through our facial expressions and body movements. These non-verbal communications play an important part when we are speaking to a person or addressing a group of people. Every effort must be made so as to keep these non-verbal communications in control. In simple terms, it is best to communicate with a positive physical presence; your body language should make you appear as a person who is both open to suggestions and approachable in time of need.

Written Communication

There is little doubt that all forms of written communication (especially electronic mail) are by far the most important and most effective mode of communication in a business. It is through the use of this mode that information can be transmitted most effectively throughout all levels of a business organisation. Written communication in the form of company policies and procedures are an important and integral part of communication between superiors and subordinates in nearly all business institutions throughout the world. In the same way, the incentive that written communication provides when dealing with external stakeholders such as customers and clients or even legal and government departments cannot be refuted or denied.

Verbal communication must translate into written communication. Words that are spoken can be forgotten; however, whatever is written is permanent in nature. In addition, written communication also provides permanency of records and serves as evidence of the events and actions that have been taken within any business organisation. They further take the form of historical records which can be used as a guide to direct the future course of a business organisation. It is for these reasons that written communication is indispensable within every business organisation.

Illustration: Son and not Sons (The Missing 'S')

In the United Kingdom, there is a bona fide government agency known as Company House which is entrusted, among other duties, to keep a watch on the creditworthiness of business companies operating within that country. It regularly oversees the performance of companies, as well as issues reports on companies, who are on the verge of bankruptcy or whose creditworthiness has declined over a certain period of time.

In the year 2009, Companies House was singularly responsible for the downfall of a 124-year-old engineering firm based in Cardiff. The name of the company in question was Taylor & Sons Ltd, and the historic business had to go into liquidity and then bankruptcy only because the Registrar of Companies of the United Kingdom had misidentified it as another company with a similar name.

On 20th February 2009, Companies House issued a letter stating that the century-old company Taylor & Sons Ltd had gone into liquidation, and therefore, it would soon be closing down permanently. Furthermore, the same information had also been shared with other credit reference agencies. While Companies House realised its mistake after just three days and informed the public that the company in question was **Taylor & Son** and not **Taylor & Sons Ltd** as earlier reported, it was too late, and the damage had been done. What followed was a cascading effect, where orders were cancelled, credit was lost and suppliers started to demand their dues.

Despite its best efforts, Taylor & Sons Ltd was unable to convince its stakeholders that it was a case of mistaken identity. The business was dealt a death blow when it lost Tata Steel, an Indian conglomerate which used to provide them with business of over £400,000 a month, and a £3,000,000 contract from the Royal National Lifeboat Institute. This led the company to close down its operations in the year 2014, directly resulting in the loss of over 250 jobs.

In a landmark judgement following its closure, the British High Court found Companies House legally responsible for the demise of Taylor & Sons Ltd. It ordered the government to pay the owners of the now-dissolved company £9 million ($17.2 million) as compensation.

You must agree it's a rather stiff penalty for missing out an **'S'.**

Improving Written Communication

The above example draws one's attention to the need to correspond carefully through written communication. When written communication is not correct, it can lead to disastrous consequences.

Know Your Audience

The very essence of a written letter is that it is a means of communicating with a specific individual or group. That is to say, it is targeted at a predefined audience. Therefore, it is equally important to use written communication in a way which is best suited to this audience. While an office letter can be short and mildly informal, when writing a similar letter to a customer or supplier, the same communication is required to be courteous and formal in nature. In fact, written communication is all about the ability to adapt to the needs of various audiences and your capacity to identify with their wavelength. It is highly recommended that the tone, style and vocabulary are in sync with the message which you want to deliver and the audience you wish to address.

The Objective of the Letter

All business communication is meant to achieve a well-defined purpose. Therefore, it is important for us to be very clear as to what that purpose or objective may be. Knowing the purpose of the written communication serves to give a sense of direction. It is essential to be clear about what the communication is expected to achieve. Asking yourself certain questions such as 'What is the need of this letter?' or 'Why is it important to write this letter?' will go a long way in the formation of a letter, which will then be able to translate your thoughts into words. Furthermore, when the objectives or goals of the written communication are clear, only then will we be in a position to effectively communicate it. The recipient will then be better able to understand our need, purpose and significance of creating such a letter or document.

Be Factual and Precise

When writing any document, there is a need to send a clear message that leaves no room for confusion. It is important to ensure that all the information in the letter or document must be factual so that it can be verified easily. As earlier stated, a letter must fulfil a verified purpose. It is important to let the recipient know what to do with the information provided. By not being clear in its purpose, the letter will lose its value and thus will not achieve its objective. Many business letters also tend to be voluminous in nature such that they continue for pages after pages. This is a bad practice; volume does not equal comprehension. Each written communication must be only as long as it can accurately communicate its message. If any other information is required, it is best to include them as separate attachments.

Maintain Proper Flow

One of the biggest mistakes when composing written communication is that they begin and end abruptly. They lack a proper flow of proceedings, which in turn leads to the message being lost. Special care should be taken to build up a letter to its ultimate end. As far as possible, every effort should be taken to avoid scripts such as roundabout sentences, large words and flowery language. In fact, every endeavour must be made to compose a concise and focused document. It is highly recommended to use short paragraphs, headings, sub-headings and even bullet points. These methods will actually allow the message and significance of the letter to be understood by the recipients more promptly and clearly.

Proofread

Once a document is ready, proofread it thoroughly. You must ensure that all the points that you wish to tackle are addressed properly and in their entirety. Special care must be taken with regard to removing all spelling, grammatical and typing mistakes. It is best to go through every paragraph individually and make corrections as and where required. Many times, we depend on software to do the checking for us; this is not a good practice. It is recommended to first print out the entire document and read it aloud. Any mistakes should be cancelled and corrected in pencil. The document should be sent to its designated recipient only when the entire document is checked in full and the corrections are incorporated.

Hire a Professional

It is common practice to find many organisations soliciting the help of professional writers for their written communication. These professional writers create, develop and authenticate almost all different types of written material for these organisations. Simply put, if an organisation is weak in their written communication, they must hire qualified writers to do that job for them. In today's day and age, there are a whole host of individuals as well as many firms which offer their services for specific prescribed fees. It is always recommended that such services should be encouraged so as to strengthen both the internal and external communication of a business organisation.

In the end, both verbal and written communication are integral and important parts of business communication. Individuals and organisations must dedicate time and effort to both encourage and improve these skills first within themselves and then transmit the same through the different levels of their own establishments.

Chapter Eight

Teamwork: Don't Create a Team; Create An Inner Circle

"Coming together is the BEGINNING.
Keeping together is PROCESS.
Working together is SUCCESS."

Henry Ford
(Founder, Ford Motor Company U.S.A)

One of the best definitions of the word 'team' is T = Together, E = Everyone, A = Achieves, M = More. If history has taught us anything, it is that no matter what business, industry or trade you come from, working together as a team gives the maximum opportunity to achieve success in your enterprise. The ability of an individual to work as a member of a team to achieve a designated goal is a highly valued and sought-after attribute by almost all organisations throughout the world.

Most certainly, within any organisation, there will be certain jobs which require individual focus and attention. However, the vast majority of work will gain substantially when it is allocated to be done by a group of employees through the formation of a team. Teamwork not only encourages the development of the individual employees but also promotes collaborations and partnerships between the various departments within an organisation. Teamwork is a crucial ingredient which recognises that when individual talents are collectively brought together and directed towards a specific direction, it leads to the realisation of the overall purpose of an organisation.

At any given point in time, there are many teams operating within an organisation. Some teams are organised to develop products, while others are organised to improve sales. Furthermore, some are involved with manufacturing and others, with research. As a result, while the formation of a team is important, it is equally vital to understand the dynamics of team building within the workplace. In fact, all successful organisations regularly spend large sums of money to improve the co-relation and coordination within their employees. It is for this reason that entrepreneurs and leaders regularly develop strategies which promote team building within their organisation. Therefore, understanding the different elements of teamwork and focusing on the diverse methods of building a team are critical for the success of any enterprise.

Illustration: The Belly and the Members

Here, to illustrate the importance of teamwork, I borrow a tale from 'Aesop's Fables' a children's story titled 'The Belly and the Members'.

It once came to be that the various members or parts of the body, more specifically the hands, the mouth, the teeth and legs, began to feel that while they were doing most of the work, the belly was getting all the food. In their opinion, they felt that the belly was a lazy and unproductive part of the body and did not deserve the amount of food it was receiving. To this effect, the disgruntled body parts called a meeting and decided to go on strike until the belly agreed to participate in an equal share of work.

To this end, the hands refused to lift the food, the mouth refused to receive it, the teeth, in turn, had no work to do. In all, the body received no food. The effect of the strike was evident in just a few days: the hands could hardly move; the mouth became dry; the legs became weak. Eventually, the entire body collapsed, and before the striking body parts realised their mistake, the whole body died.

This story teaches us two very important aspects of teamwork. First, for any organisation to succeed, all its separate parts, such as different departments, employees and stakeholders, must work together as a cohesive unit. The second and most important aspect is that no single department, stakeholder or individual will contribute in equal measure to the success of an organisation. Simply put, the success of an organisation is dependant on the participation of all levels of management, each contributing their part at different levels and in different proportions to the overall success of the organisation.

Benefits of Teamwork

There is little doubt that there are many measurable benefits of teamwork within an organisation. Furthermore, there are various types of literature available in various forms of media throughout the world to the same effect. However, I found it only prudent to take the opportunity to mention certain unique benefits which, although are well known, are rarely discussed.

Builds Internal Trust

Working together encourages members of an organisation to build trust and confidence between each other. As different departments are made of many diverse people, this trust and belief within these individuals translate into better reliance, trust and confidence between the various departments as well. It is true also that there will still remain some employees within an organisation who, despite all the efforts of the management of the organisation, will still be unable to accept the concept of working together as a team. For individuals such as these, the presence and perseverance of the other team members who promote the collective spirit of working together further act as a catalyst to modify their working style towards a more collaborative approach.

In simple terms, one of the greatest advantages of an effective team is that it unites and solidifies the working of internal departments within an institution. This internal unity and strength lead to a direct correlation in not only how the organisation conducts its dealing in the external world but, more importantly, also reflects the way the institution is perceived by the business community in general.

Teamwork Encourages Collective Accountability

One of the hidden benefits of teamwork is that it encourages collective accountability. Since all members are collectively responsible for the performance of the team, this encourages the team to come up with more creative and innovative solutions. The threat of being singularly responsible is diminished, and it is seen that almost all members become more collaborative and accommodative to the ideas and suggestions of the other team members. Each team member quickly realises that the performance of each individual reflects on the team as a whole. In fact, each member competes with the other members to generate a more researched and more scrutinised solution.

This being said, this type of collective accountability is sometimes seen to discourage certain team members from participating wholeheartedly. In fact, certain team members are also seen to pass on their work allocation to other more active members. It is in times such as these that the top management must step in so as to clearly promote the idea that the effort of teamwork is not a philosophical goal but an intrinsic part of the organisation's work culture. More importantly, members who are seen to regularly evade their responsibility should be made well aware that while the team is collectively responsible for its performance, the rewards for the success of the team are always divided on the basis of the individual contribution of each team member. Thus, your reward will only be equal to the extent of the effort of your own contribution.

Improves Communication Skills

Communication is one of the key aspects through which a team is successful. It is important that a team member regularly communicates and consults with the key members of the team on a customary basis. It is an essential duty for the leader of a team to act as an effective conduit so as to encourage the sharing of information to all the members of the team. Each member of the team must be made to realise that while they are handling separate areas of the job at hand, it is their duty to constantly update each other on their progress as well as any problems which may be impeding them in the completion of their task.

It is also crucial that given the rapid advances made in communication technology in the form of email, WhatsApp, video conferencing and other such platforms, it is essential that all team members should be brought up to date on the various technologies available at their disposal. The objective here is that should the need arise, all team members are able to connect and interact with each other, irrespective of the time or their geographic location.

Development of New Leaders

It is the desire of every team member to be allocated as the leader of a team. However, to lead a team, a person must have the correct perspective and experience to do so. It is the attempt of every organisation to allocate team members in the hope that they may be potential leaders in the future. To this effect, the selection of a person to a specific team, their job allocation as well as their performance are all essential criteria which are constantly recorded by the senior management of the organisation.

Being a leader does not mean that you are allowed to throw your weight around. In fact, it is the role of a team leader to develop and guide his team members to achieve a predetermined goal or objective. Some team members do not realise that they are being groomed for a better prospect in the future. In many cases, the difference between a good and a great leader comes down to simple experience. Therefore, once the senior management identifies an employee as a potential leadership prospect, they will set him or her on a path where the individual will be given an opportunity to gain valuable experience in various management positions in different departments of the organisation in rapid succession. Furthermore, it is also commonplace to see potential leaders being sent to different geographical areas of the world, and sometimes they are offered training programmes to better enhance their ability and confidence. All these steps are taken by an organisation so that there is a ready base of new leaders to take over from the already established leaders as and when the appropriate time comes to pass.

Increases Efficiency and Reduces Cost

Typically, when a group of people work together to achieve a common goal, they do so in a more efficient way. Efficiency increases as the responsibility of an individual team member will usually relate to their specific ability and skill set. An individual team member is allocated and responsible only for a small part of the overall objective and goal. Since, in most cases, that role is clearly defined, a team member will increase focus on the job at hand; this leads to the improvement of their own efficiency, in turn leading to the improvement of the overall efficiency of the group as a whole.

Furthermore, since the group consists of individuals with their own specialisation, most of the problems or obstacles are resolved in-house. There is rarely a need to bring in an outside consultant or agency. This allows the goals of an organisation to be achieved at a reduced cost. To put it simply, rather than having four individuals sitting in four different corners of the organisation, if these individuals are able to communicate with each other, they together can not only share their ideas and suggestion but can help each other in achieving their common goals more efficiently and at a reduced cost to the organisation.

Steps for Building an Effective Team

Build a Pool of Human Resource

In any organisation, there will be different situations which will be required to be solved through the formation of a team. In modern business organisations, a team consists of different individuals bringing their own expertise to a business situation or occurrence. To this effect, no one team will be a perfect fit for all the situations. It is, therefore, a proven practice to create a pool of individuals who can be brought together at any point of time to solve or deal with any unique situation which may transpire in the day to day working of the organisation. This type of flexible team system provides a great advantage in saving both time and money in establishments where it is implemented.

Understanding each Team Member's Strengths

An effective business leader or entrepreneur will make a genuine effort to get to know each of the individuals in his organisation. They will spend a large amount of time assessing the capabilities of their employees, paying special attention to their strengths and weaknesses and also, more importantly, to their expertise and competencies in terms of specific difficult problems at their position within the organisation. It is every leader's responsibility to know how best any employee is to be motivated so as to allow them to achieve the best result for themselves and the organisation they serve.

Build Relationships Between your Employees

An equally important responsibility of any business leader or entrepreneur is to facilitate a healthy and cooperative environment between different team members. It is eventually the cohesiveness of the individuals working together which will be directly responsible for the end result. It is the primary duty of a leader to listen carefully to both sides of an argument and guide the discussion to its natural end. Each individual team member should be encouraged to put forth his point of view but also be encouraged to listen to the views of his or her other team members. An effective method of doing this is to encourage team-building exercises and brainstorming sessions so as to effectively empower all team members to come up with new and innovative solutions to different problems.

Set Clear Team Goals

All teams are set up to achieve specific goals. It is the sole responsibility of the top management to clearly define what the team is meant to achieve. It is essential that all parameters be discussed thoroughly and all doubts be cleared up in a systematic method. It is important to convey the role of each team member and address their contribution to the team. Furthermore, it is also essential to reach a consensus within the predefined parameters and guarantee the result within a specific time period. It is a prudent practice to delegate a clearly defined responsibility to each and every team member and to hold them accountable to that specified task. In this way, it allows the senior management to accurately gauge the individual team member's talent as well as their overall contribution to the team.

Deputation of Team Leader

One of the most common problems which arises in a team is that, sometimes, all team members stake their contention for the leadership position. To this effect, the essence of the team and their correlation and coordination are disrupted. To avoid such a situation, it is important to delegate the role of team leader at the very beginning of the team formation process. It should be clearly declared to all members of the team that the decision of the team leader is final and irrevocable. This clear affirmation of the leadership role also gives strength to the deputed leader to take independent decisions. However, more importantly, it allows the team leader a free hand in all aspects of the specified goal set by the top management. This, in turn, allows all members of the team to focus on their delegated task and, therefore, perform to their best abilities to achieve their goal together.

Communication

The three pillars of any team are trust, transparency and communication. Every effort must be made to create an atmosphere where ideas and information are shared freely. Each team member must be encouraged to share their individual thoughts on the matter at hand. Special care must be taken so that no team member is ridiculed or humiliated, no matter how insignificant their suggestion may seem. This act of constant free communication will help to ensure that all team members are on a common platform and are moving towards the achievement of a common result.

Promote Decisions Through Consensus

One of the key reasons for the success of any team leader is their ability to bring consensus between his team members. While it is true that building consensus is a time-consuming process, it ultimately leads to more informed decisions, resulting in greater productivity and better results for the organisation. It is further important to be aware of false consensus, and therefore, it is paramount to give each team member adequate time to both present and seek clarification on various issues within the proposed decision. In the end, the key advantage of promoting consensus decision is that it secures every team member's commitment and accountability towards the final decision implemented by the organisation.

Reward Handsomely

This is perhaps an area which is not given much importance in the Indian corporate scene. Any individual or team can be greatly motivated if the rewards of achieving the desired result are enhanced to a great extent. A reward for a job well done must go beyond a simple promotion or a nominal salary increase. Business leaders and entrepreneurs are regularly seen to reward their key employees with all sorts of fabulous incentives to motivate them to give their best performance. This practice of rewarding the achievements of an individual or team greatly enhances the confidence and self-belief of all the members of the organisation. Thus, it acts to motivate the other members of the organisation to improve their own performance and further encourages them to remain loyal to the organisation for a long time.

In conclusion, teamwork provides many organisations with several benefits and advantages. Close collaboration has, in fact, been one of the chief hallmarks of human achievement. Therefore, all business leaders and entrepreneurs firmly believe that a good and efficient team will contribute to the success of their organisation. They are regularly seen promoting the formation of teams to deal with the various issues which arise both internally and externally within their organisation.

Team-Building Theory

To improve the understanding of the dynamics of team building, it is essential to spend some time examining a variety of team-building theories. While there are many theories available on the subject, my personal favourite is Tuckman's theory, which has been presented below:

Tuckman's Theory

Bruce Wayne Tuckman (November –4, 1938 – March 13, 2016) was a psychology professor who specialised in the theory of group dynamics. In 1965, he published a revolutionary theory known as 'Tuckman's stages of group development'. This, for the first time, attempted to define specific parameters which played an integral part in the dynamics of a group of individuals working towards the achievement of a specific goal or objective. One of the major reasons that Tuckman's theory was so well received by both academicians and the business community alike was that it proved simple to understand and effortless to implement.

His original theory was published in the year 1965 and consisted of four stages: forming, storming, norming and performing. In 1977, he improved this theory by adding a fifth stage, adjourning.

Forming – Stage 1

The first stage or **forming stage** primarily exists at a time when a new team has just been formed for the first time. It is that period when each of the individuals who have been put together is getting to know each other. In most cases, in this stage, the group leader for the task at hand has been appointed. It is the time when job roles are defined and allocated to all the team members. Since this an occasion of uncertainty, it is the duty of the leader to be prepared to answer and clarify any questions which the team may put to him or her. It is essential for the leader to clearly communicate the team's purpose, objectives and what is expected from the team as a whole. Since this is the initial stage, in most cases, there will be no well-defined structure or process or boundaries in terms of the working of the team. It is the leader who must draw on his or her experience and ability to design and implement a viable environment in which the team is to operate.

Storming – Stage 2

The second stage or **storming stage** is that period of time when different team members will attempt to establish their dominance or influence on the team. Power struggles are commonplace in this stage. In fact, there may be cases where certain team members may wish to replace the appointed leader and appoint themselves in that position. One of the major reasons for this situation to arise is that while there may be clarity of purpose, many doubts will remain even at this stage. The most challenging issues for the leader will be to establish his or her authority over the team and focus the team's effort towards the predefined goals and objectives through consensus and agreement.

Norming – Stage 3

In the **norming stage** or third stage, the leadership issue has been resolved. The role and responsibility of each and every team member are clear and well defined. The team begins to respond and perform its duties through the instruction of the appointed leader. The decision process becomes well defined, and almost all decisions are made through consensus and mutual agreement. The most important feature of this stage is that the team discusses and implements both its working style and implementation system in consultation with each other. It is common to find that the team grows to admire and respect the various contributions of their team members as well as the appointed leader. Most importantly, the individual members begin to function as a single unified group to achieve the aims and objectives which had been their purpose from the very beginning.

Performing – Stage 4

In the **performing stage** or fourth stage, the team knows clearly what it hopes to achieve and is aware, to a great extent, of what is required to achieve those aims and objectives. The team now performs as a coercive single-minded entity. There is an overwhelming focus on the tasks which are to be achieved. The team now makes most of its decisions based on the criteria which are agreed through consensus of the team; disagreements, if any, are resolved through discussion. The final outcomes and decisions are subject to the final approval of the team leader. The team also reaches a point of self-belief, where it is able to make most of the decisions on its own. However, as the situation arises, they refer to the team leaders for their guidance and support. In fact, there is a great degree of autonomy within the team, and its members are seen to work towards their goals and objectives by regularly improving and upgrading their internal system and processes within the team dynamics.

Team members connect on a personal level and are seen to look out for each other's interest. In fact, the team reaches a stage where its members no longer need to be instructed or even assisted in their tasks. The leaders reach a position where their duty is to strategically manoeuvre all the resources at their disposal to the achievement of the ultimate goal or objective.

Adjourning – Stage 5

The last stage or the **adjourning stage** comes when the team has achieved the goals and objectives for which it was set up. At this stage, the team is dissolved and its team members either go back to their old functions or are reassigned to other departments within the organisation. It is important here for the team leader to recognise individual team members for their contribution and celebrate the achievements of the team. In some cases, some team members may feel uncertain and insecure about their future prospects. It is the duty of the team leader as well as the leadership of that organisation to negate such effects with an appropriate plan for the reintegration of the team members within the main organisation.

In conclusion, the ability of an entrepreneur or leader to work with a team is an essential requirement to achieve success in the business realm. So, the importance of fostering a healthy and productive environment within an organisation should not be taken lightly. In the end, teamwork stands at the centre of all human accomplishment. It is important to realise its need, and care should be taken to encourage it in all your future undertakings.

Chapter Nine

Conflict Resolution in the Workplace: the *Skilled Touch* of Compromise

"If we manage conflict constructively,
We harness its energy for creativity and development."

Kenneth Kaye
(American Psychologist and Writer)

Every business organisation consists of individuals with different beliefs, distinctive backgrounds, varied values and diverse attitudes. That being said, when such group diversity exists in a single organisation, there is bound to be disagreements, which will invariably lead to conflicts. Conflicts in the workplace are an irrefutable reality in the modern business world. If left unresolved, they can lead to many undesirable situations and results within an organisation.

As a business leader, it becomes important to not only identify the possible areas of conflict but also resolve them effectively in a time-bound manner. Mastering the fundamentals of conflict resolution enables an individual to not only become a better team player but also an improved decision-maker and superior leader. When a conflict at the workplace is resolved in a systematic and positive manner, it leads to a direct improvement in the personal and professional relationships between co-workers and the leadership. A positive resolution to a conflict in the workplace not only saves both time and resources, it further improves productivity and helps in realigning the focus back towards the original objectives of the organisation. Therefore, it is essential that both entrepreneurs and leaders must possess the required prerequisite knowledge of the possible theories and practices of resolving conflict as and when they arise within their organisations.

Illustration: Maruti Udyog Limited vs Suzuki Motors Corporation

Suzuki Motors Corporation entered India in 1981 through the incorporation of Maruti Udyog Limited, a joint venture company between itself and the Government of India. The aim of the joint venture was to produce a new passenger car well within the reach of the common man. At the initial stage, Suzuki Motors Corporation held 26% of the share within the newly formed Maruti Udyog Limited. By the year 1992, both Suzuki Motors Corporation and the Government of India had become equal partners, each holding an equal 50% of Maruti Udyog Limited. As per an agreement between the partners, it was decided that each partner would take turns in appointing their choice for the post of the managing director of Maruti Udyog Limited.

Therefore, in 1992, the Suzuki Motors Corporation nominee R.C. Bhargava, who was due to retire the same year, was duly appointed as the managing director and was granted an extension of five years. The clear and mutual understanding was that on the retirement of R.C. Bhargava, the Government of India would nominate its nominee to the post. However, it seemed that R.C. Bhargava had other ideas, and during his tenure, he brought in a former bureaucrat and rank outsider by the name of Jagdish Khattar and appointed him as an officer on special duty and began to train him as his future successor.

In 1997, as per the arrangement, it was time for the Government of India to appoint its nominee. Murasoli Maran, the then industries minister, nominated R.S.S.L.N. Bhaskarudu to the post of managing director. This time, however, Suzuki Motors Corporation objected to this appointment and appeared to push the candidature of Jagdish Khattar for the post of managing director. In fact, Suzuki Motors Corporation further demanded the resignation of R.S.S.L.N. Bhaskarudu, claiming that his appointment was illegal, since five of the nine directors of the Maruti Udyog Limited board, who constituted the majority of the board, had strongly objected to his appointment on the grounds that he was incompetent and unsuitable for the post of managing director. The Government of India, citing the 1992 agreement and the clauses contained therein, refused to do so and summarily declined the proposal outright.

The disagreement reached a flashpoint in the Annual General Meeting held on September 22, 1997, where representatives of both Suzuki Motors Corporation and the Government of India exchanged allegations and counter-allegations between each other and even nearly came close to physically assaulting each other. After the tempers were calmed down, the appointment of R.S.S.L.N. Bhaskarudu was put to a floor test, which proved equal once more. At this point of time, Prabir Sengupta, the chairman of Maruti Udyog Limited, a Government of India nominee, used his casting vote and ratified the appointment of R.S.S.L.N. Bhaskarudu to the post of managing director.

This infuriated the representatives of Suzuki Motors Corporation further, and they immediately passed a no-confidence motion against Prabir Sengupta and proposed the name of Yoshio Saito for the post of chairman. The Government of India, in turn, refused this proposal and backed Prabir Sengupta, further stating that he would be allowed to continue his tenure as chairman and demit his office only in the year 2000, as he was entitled to do. Suzuki Motors Corporation, to further apply pressure on the Government of India, then lodged an arbitration petition against R.S.S.L.N. Bhaskarudu's appointment in the International Court of Arbitration.

This serious conflict perhaps would have never come to an end, should fate not have intervened to resolve it. In 1998, India held its 12th Lok Sabha elections and a new political party formed the next government. The new government was proactive in seeking a solution for the Maruti Udyog Limited dispute. In the year 1999, a solution was finally reached. As per the settlement terms, S.S.L.N. Bhaskarudu would resign from his post as managing director, a full two years before scheduled. The Suzuki Motors Corporation nominee, Jagdish Khattar, would take his place. Additionally, Prabir Sengupta, the incumbent chairman, was also replaced by Yoshio Saito as chairman.

Now, it is clear that Suzuki Motors Corporation emerged as the clear victor, as it was able to acquire both the posts in dispute for its nominees. However, this victory was greatly influenced by the fact that the new government which had come to power had resolved to disinvest its holding in Maruti Udyog Limited. To that effect, the Government of India divested its complete holding in Maruti Udyog Limited in two phases. The first phase was completed by December 2001, and the second and final phase was completed a year later. Once more, Suzuki Motors Corporation was able to acquire a substantial portion of the shares divested. The final result was that for all intents and purposes, Maruti Udyog Limited had ceased to exist and had now become a fully owned subsidiary of Suzuki Motors Corporation.

One of the most important and evident conclusions which can be drawn from the illustration above is the difference in the view and style adopted by the two governments to resolve the conflict. While the earlier government showed aggression and confrontation in its temperament and approach towards the issue, the new government seemed more amicable and passive in its approach. Therefore, it is essential to realise that there are various conflict resolution styles available to entrepreneurs and business leaders to adopt when they are faced with a similar situation within their organisation.

For that reason, it is critical to have knowledge with regard to the different conflict resolution styles currently most utilised on a regular basis in business organisations throughout the world.

Different Styles of Conflict Resolution

The Avoidance Style

The avoidance style is comparable to a wait-and-watch policy. It is characterised by a system which hopes that the conflict will get resolved by itself over a period of time. Individuals who utilise this style are extremely hazardous to their organisations. In most cases, their inaction causes even the smallest problems and situations to reach alarming and dangerous proportions. Individuals of this style are seen to be self-serving and are not remotely concerned about the effect of their actions on their colleagues and organisation. Such individuals should be identified and dealt with firmly and should be eased out of the organisation.

The Yielding Style

The yielding style is also known as the **accommodating** style. In this approach, it is common for one of the parties to allow the other party to have its way in order to maintain the relationship. This passive approach is common when individuals derive personal satisfaction in the success of the other individual; when faced with a situation of conflict, the individual will agree with the other individual on the grounds that it will maintain the same level of peace and harmony which had existed before the conflict began. In a business situation, however, in more cases than not, the individual doing the yielding and accommodating will harbour feelings of resentment, which are a direct consequence of his or her being left out of the decision-making process.

The Competitive Conflict Style

The competitive style, also known as the **fighting** style or **forcing** style, is usually seen when one of the parties in a conflict refuses to back down and stands their ground. To this effect, they are willing to do anything and everything to win the conflict. They see the conflict as a 'win or lose' and are usually adamant for the other party to agree to their point of view. In fact, in this style, it is common to see the aggressive party use accusations, insults and even the threat of violence to achieve a dominant position. This style may offer rewards in the short term but may also be harmful to the business in the future. However, in certain rare cases where a leader is of the opinion that his point of view is the most effective and suitable solution to a problem, they may intervene by using their authority and have the final word.

The Compromising Conflict Style

The compromising style, also known as the **bargaining** style or **conciliation** style, is usually seen when both the parties in a conflict agree to look for a common ground to resolve their differences in viewpoints. This style requires great courage and consideration from both sides. Each group agrees to give up certain core demands and, in turn, offer certain relaxations to the other side. In simple terms, both parties agree to meet other **'halfway'** so that the conflict is resolved in an advantageous position to all concerned. Each party does this in the hope that the other side will put a fair value on their concerns and will, therefore, agree to an amicable solution to the conflict. One of the greatest advantages of this style is that it promotes understanding and goodwill between the parties, which may pave the way for further cooperation in the future.

The Collaborating Conflict Style

The collaborating style, also known as the **integration** style or **cooperation** style, is perhaps the most desired yet most difficult style to adopt in resolving a conflict. In this approach, both parties are aware of the substantial gains and rewards which they will receive if the conflict is amicably resolved. To this effect, they devote their time and effort to resolve each and every point of disagreement between each other. In almost all cases, both parties have to suggest innovative solutions which have to be agreed upon by all concerned parties without any concessions and dispensations. This style creates a 'win-win' solution for both the disputing parties. However, this style is extremely time-consuming and puts an unfair strain on the resources of both parties. Therefore, the collaborating style is used only in the rarest of instances.

In the business world, the best approach is usually a combination of two or more of the conflict resolution styles discussed. It is important to match both the style and approach to the situation as and how required. This being said, **four key variables** play an essential part in determining which conflict management style is likely to be the most effective. They are:

Time Pressure

Time is a valuable resource and is limited in nature. Time spent on resolving any conflict within an organisation is a waste of that priceless resource. Entrepreneurs and business leaders are well aware that there is never enough time for resolving a conflict. Time exerts its own pressure on conflict situations. In fact, if time were not an important factor, most conflicts would never be resolved. Therefore, it is the availability of time which is the single most important factor to take into consideration when choosing a conflict resolution style and approach.

Issue Importance

The importance or priority of any issue to any one of the two parties significantly affects the importance of the way they approach the conflict. If an issue is not that relevant to either party, they will spend less time and may even agree to the solution offered without putting up any resistance. On the other hand, if an issue holds great importance, the concerned party will prolong the conflict until the same is resolved as per their needs and desire. In fact, most protracted conflicts are fought around a small number of core issues. Therefore, the style of approach by the concerned party is of great consequence.

Relationship Importance

The importance of the relationship that the two parties involved in a conflict share is also a crucial factor in selecting a style of conflict resolution. When conflicts arise within an organisation, in most cases, the two parties are in some way attached to each other; they may have collaborated in other areas for the organisation. The conflicting parties are, after all, colleagues, peers or even contemporaries working in the same or different departments of the same organisation. In this case, it is important to resolve the conflict in a mutually supportive and beneficial nature. Special care should be taken to strengthen the relationship between the two parties so that they continue to partner with each other in the future collaborations of the organisation.

Relative Power

In any conflict, the amount of power which one party of the dispute has, in comparison to the other, plays an important part in the ultimate result of the dispute. If a conflict is to be resolved in an honest and fair way, there must be a formal system in place, where parties involved in the dispute are free to share their side of events. When such a system is put in place, it allows for the dispute to be resolved correctly and fairly. It, more importantly, also promotes to both the parties that their views and observations will be considered and the best solution will be offered. In almost all cases, the dispute is resolved in an amicable method, which further strengthens the bond between the disputing parties.

In conclusion, it is important to remember that while conflicts will inevitably arise between people in an organisation, it is the duty of the leadership to identify and resolve a conflict effectively and quickly. Special care must be taken to resolve the underlying issues in a concise and positive manner. Resolving conflict in this way results in the improvement of professional and personal relationships in a positive manner within an organisation. In fact, most entrepreneurs and business leaders have mastered a large number of well-defined fundamental conflict resolution skills. These skills have enabled them to become a better decision-maker, co-worker and even mentor to their employees.

Effective Strategies in Resolving Conflict at the Workplace

1. Acknowledge the Problem

The first step in resolving conflict at the workplace is acknowledging that a conflict exists. It is also true that conflict arises only when the smaller issues within an organisation are not resolved. It is this build-up of various smaller issues which is the foundation of the larger conflict. Many times, it is these smaller issues which are the precursors to an imminent conflict at the workplace. Leaders within the organisation must train themselves to recognise these signals and take proactive steps to diffuse the same. Therefore, essentially, a conflict resolution technique can be applied to resolve a conflict only when the conflict is identified.

2. Gather Information

The second step is to gather as much information as possible on the real issues of the conflict. It is essential to clearly identify all the events and parties involved in the conflict. Special care must be taken to comprehend how the issues identified affect both the parties involved in the conflict. It is important to take enough time and sort out relevant and important information which may help resolve the conflict in an amicable manner. In almost all organisations, there is a clear directive that should any conflict arise, it must be solved in the shortest and most reasonable way possible. Many times, leaders may form a team of individuals to look into the matter and provide them with a composite brief on the chain of events leading up to the conflict. To achieve this, it is essential to gather information in a clear and precise manner so that the real issues may be identified and then rectified on a real-time and immediate basis.

3. Establish Guidelines

It is essential that all matters relating to a conflict must be resolved in a proper and well-defined manner. It, therefore, becomes necessary to establish rules and guidelines to this effect. This is essentially to communicate to both the conflicting parties on the seriousness of the issue. Furthermore, it adequately demonstrates the intention of the leadership to resolve the same in a free and fair manner. Once these guidelines are established, all the parties involved must agree to accept this formal system of prescribed rules and regulation within which the meeting is held. The objective is to get both the parties to give a fair hearing to each other's perspective. More importantly, it is to push for an amicable solution, as far as possible, which is agreed and settled on by both the parties themselves, making it clear that should any party violate the terms and conditions agreed upon, the punishment for their actions will be severe.

4. Determine the Medium

While the most preferred medium of addressing a conflict in the workplace is a meeting, certain situations may warrant a different medium. In fact, many business leaders are now regularly seen to prefer an informal setting. To this end, conflicts are being resolved outside the office over activities such as a coffee, lunches or even through casual walks. This change in the scenario has gained a preference due to the disappearance of the formal hierarchy system which persisted in the past. Choosing the correct medium plays an integral role in encouraging the parties in conflict to share their different points of view and encourages a solution through discussion. At the first instance, almost all organisations prefer to use an informal setting, where both parties are encouraged to solve their issues between themselves. When this effort fails, an organisation usually has no other option but to resolve the situation in a more traditional setting through a formal meeting.

5. Keep the Communication Open

One of the key requirements for effective conflict resolution is to ensure that all parties involved have a meaningful discussion. It is extremely important to let each of the parties have their complete say in the matter so that even the smallest points of dispute are brought out for discussion. When the lines of communication are open, the core issues of the conflict are revealed. It is essential to frame a discussion in a way that all the chain of events is discussed in a point to point format. Special care is to be taken to divide these points on the basis of their importance. Then each point or issue is raised in the sequence of its priority. It is at this time that each issue should be discussed thoroughly and in its entirety. Furthermore, the next issue should be taken up for discussion only when the issue at hand is resolved completely. In essence, almost all conflicts within an organisation can be resolved through communication. Therefore, it is essential to introduce a system where the employees can freely exchange and propose their ideas, suggestions and solutions for the betterment of the organisation.

6. Repeat back your Understanding of the Issues

In some cases, one party involved in the conflict may not be able to effectively communicate their view on a critical issue. Or, worse still, they communicate their views in such a way that it is misunderstood by the other party. It is primarily for this reason that all meetings to resolve conflict are **tripartite in nature.** That is to say, there are the two parties of the conflict and then the third individual or team are representatives of the leadership of the organisation, referred to as the mediators. It is the duty of these mediators to make sure that the meeting is resolved in a composed and peaceful manner. More importantly, they are responsible to see that the ideas and suggestions are communicated, shared and understood by both the parties involved within the dispute. Furthermore, the mediators act as a channel for top leadership, regularly updating them on all that transpires within the meeting, allowing them to intervene and guide the conflict to a mutually rewarding result.

7. Act Decisively

Once all the information has been gathered and all the individuals involved in the conflict are interviewed and their viewpoints have been shared, it is time to act decisively. It is the time when those at fault are clearly identified and reprimanded for their mistakes. To this effect, the reprimand may come in the form of a stern warning or even termination from the organisation. The leadership of any organisation, when dealing with conflict, cannot be seen as weak or silent when it comes time to dole out the punishment to the guilty parties. It is imperative to be proactive and censure those at fault. In this way, the leadership is able to send a clear message throughout the whole organisation that it does not appreciate conflicts in the workplace and is more than willing to deal with such matter with a firm hand.

8. Record the Final Decision for Future Conflicts

After the final decision has been taken on the resolution of the conflict, it is prudent to communicate the same throughout the entire organisation. Doing this has a twofold effect: The first is that it not only communicates the chain of events which led to the conflict but also clearly identifies the party at fault and details the action taken by the top leadership of the organisation. The second and perhaps most important effect is that it creates a permanent record which is readily available to potential leaders of the organisation to utilise as a reference in the future.

In conclusion, conflict at the workplace is a reality, and when it arises, it affects the functioning of the organisation. The core importance of any conflict resolution is the restoring of the cordial relationship between the conflicting parties. It is for this reason alone that business leaders regularly update their knowledge on the various conflict resolution techniques. One thing is clear: the conflict will not go away by itself and will only get worse if ignored. Therefore, it is essential to have procedures in place to deal with it in a fair and effective manner.

Chapter Ten

Motivation The Transfer of Ownership

"Motivation is the art of getting people to do
What you want them to do because they want to do it."

Dwight D. Eisenhower
(American Army General and Former President of the United States of America)

Successful companies are built on the shoulders of their employees. It is the duty of every entrepreneur and business leader to accept this fact. When companies are in their nascent stage, it is easy for an individual or small group of people to administrate the day to day functioning of an organisation. However, when the same organisation grows, it becomes necessary to hire more employees. These new employees are expected to work together and contribute to the growth of the organisation. Two of the most important factors that are responsible for the growth of the organisation are the motivation and sense of ownership which are shared between the leader and his small group. Now, once the organisation has become larger, it is important that the same motivation is transferred to the new employees so that the new employees will also share a sense of ownership for the organisation. This, in turn, will stimulate them to work together and give their best for the betterment of their organisation. In simple terms, the dreams and aspirations of the creators of the original organisation must be transferred to the new employees

Entrepreneurs and business leaders are well aware of the importance of creating an environment within the organisation in which employees are motivated to give their best performance. In simple terms, employees must be encouraged to improve themselves such that they become invaluable assets to the organisation. All employees are individuals first, and as such, all individuals are different and are motivated by different things. Therefore, it should not come as a surprise that it is essential to gain a deep and comprehensive understanding of what motivates each and every individual employee within the organisation.

Illustration: McDonald's Olympic Champion Crew

McDonald's is a globally renowned fast-food company, serving over 69 million customers in over 100 countries on a daily basis. It was estimated as of 2016 that McDonald's was the second-largest employer in the world, with approximately 1.5 million employees. In fact, it has also been reported that in the United States of America, one out of every eight workers at some time or the other has been an employee for the McDonald's corporation.

The McDonald's corporation is well aware that one of the major reasons for its success is the performance of its employees. They continuously introduce new and exciting schemes for their employees so as to keep them motivated to perform their duties to the best of their abilities.

One such innovative and successful scheme was the **Olympic Champion Crew Initiative.** This scheme came about when McDonald's was able to successfully bid to become the official restaurant of the 2012 Olympic and Paralympics Games being held in London. Given the scale of the event, McDonald's decided to construct a 3000 square metre restaurant to serve the over three million people expected to visit during the games. However, the most daunting challenge was to select the over 2000 McDonald's staff who would provide service to the visitors during the games.

The **Olympic Champion Crew Initiative** was launched in January 2011 and encompassed all the 1200 restaurants operating within the United Kingdom. The objective of this scheme was to motivate the staff to be selected to serve in one of the four restaurants during the Olympic and Paralympics Games. The modus operandi was quite simple: in the run-up to the games, each restaurant would identify its top performer aka Olympic Champion every month. Each monthly top performer was rewarded with an Olympic goody bag which contained various Olympic Games-themed gifts. Out of these ten top performers, the best five were nominated for the second stage of the programme. In the second stage, many different skill assessments were done, and out of these, the top 2500 employees were selected to serve at the venue of the Olympic Games.

These selected staff members were rewarded with an all-expenses package, which included free lodging and boarding in a luxurious London hotel and a whole host of programmes which encouraged team-building exercises and even well-organised tours of London. In the words of Neal Blackshire, one of the top managers within the McDonald's organisation, "It took the Olympic element to really inject that extra enthusiasm. Obviously, the ability to have those ambassadors to come back from the Olympic Park, being able to talk about the hotel setup and all the other things we did to look after them away from actually working in the restaurant, really is more powerful than any number of booklets, videos and face-to-face meetings."

Furthermore, due to the grand success of this programme, McDonald's followed and introduced a similar program at the FIFA World Cup 2014. Firmly establishing the importance of such activities and schemes is an integral part of keeping employees motivated within their organisation. In fact, McDonald's has gone ahead and introduced many more such motivation and recognition schemes for its employees throughout the globe. Such has been the positive result of these initiatives that McDonald's regularly finds itself featured as one of the top employee-friendly companies throughout the world.

In simple terms, McDonald's draws on the strength of these incentive programmes to upgrade their training programmes. At the same time, they keep a firm lookout for those employees who can be trained to become future leaders within the organisation, thus, in turn, securing for their employees a healthy work environment. This allows them to gain a continuous and robust competitive advantage over its rivals.

Self-Motivation at Work

Self-motivation is an individualistic psychological course of action which allows entrepreneurs and business leaders alike to accomplish their goals and desires. It is the first and most important step in motivating both employees as well as colleagues at the workplace. An integral part of self-motivation is the belief in one's own abilities and, more importantly, the correct attitude to get any job finished successfully. Self-motivation can be achieved by any individual if they are willing to commit to a programme of self-discovery and have the prerequisite patience to accept that it is a lifelong commitment. It, therefore, should come as no surprise that to motivate others at the workplace, the entrepreneur or business leader must be first and foremost motivated themselves. This self-motivation can be achieved by inculcating certain changes within the approach an individual undertakes at their workplace. Some of these are discussed below:

1. Be Passionate About Your Work

When any person is passionate about their work, it is bound to inspire and encourage the people around them. A common attribute of every entrepreneur and business leader is that they do what they enjoy doing. Their work is not an occupation—in fact, far from it. Their work is a manifestation of their desire to live a fulfilling life. They measure their performance on the merit of the contributions they bring to the workplace. They perceive every obstacle and problem as a learning opportunity. Their passion is, in fact, a strength which allows them to recognise the larger benefit and impact their work has on their organisation and community as a whole. Therefore, persons who are passionate about their craft are always motivated and strive to automatically give their best for their organisation without any expectation of reward or recognition.

2. Be Accountable for Your Work

In a workplace environment, it is commonly seen that when a project goes well, the credit is shared by the team. However, when a project fails or is unsuccessful, everyone in the team begins to point fingers and is on the lookout to assign the blame to others. This can be a very annoying time for an individual. On the other hand, it is times like these that define the leadership qualities of a person. It is a prudent practice that each individual of the team should reflect and re-examine for themselves their contributions to the project and discover what went wrong and how it may have contributed to the failure of the project.

If that mistake has been made by you, you must stand accountable for your mistakes. This is not an easy thing to do; such is human nature that your mind will suggest many ways to avoid doing just that. However, your strength and confidence increase when **you accept your mistake, learn from it, rectify the same** and reassure yourself to **pass on the knowledge** to your subordinates so that they do not make that same mistake. Therefore, with every job or work that you undertake, you are accountable for it, irrespective of the fact that it turned out to be a success or failure.

3. Spend Time in Improving Yourself

If you want to become a leader, you must invest time in self-improvement. Personal growth is only achieved outside an individual's comfort zone. While it is also true that your experience at the workplace will continue to mould your character and ability with the passage of time, it is also imperative that an individual must look out for other resources to achieve this. Simple things such as reading books and journals on the appropriate subject, attending conferences and seminars or even perhaps taking short-term educational courses will play a great role in enhancing a person's self-worth, not only in his or her own eyes but will further enhance their net worth to their organisation.

4. Follow the Leader

One of the best-recommended techniques to remain self-motivated is to look up and follow in the footsteps of a leader. Enhance your attitude by finding and following leaders you would like to emulate. Choose those leaders who inspire you and can influence a positive change within you. Learn and follow their experiences, decisions, trials and triumphs and use the events in their lives to motivate yourself to challenge your boundaries and achieve more than your pre-planned goals.

5. Be Optimistic

Having an optimistic mindset is also an essential characteristic in the workplace. It is necessary that an individual must first believe in the successful outcome of his job. While it is perfectly normal for a person to have a certain level of anxiety at the workplace due to their apprehension about the final result of their performance, it becomes important to do away with feelings and emotions of uncertainty, worry or even fear of failure. This is because feelings, either negative or positive, are extremely contagious and spread rapidly within an organisation. Therefore, an individual must choose to remain constructive and have a positive outlook, no matter what situations they may have to face at their workplace. Optimism is an effective weapon which reinforces self-belief during times of difficulty. Individuals who are optimistic act as beacons of hope and inspire their fellow workers to remain focused and confident of the long-term perspectives of their organisation. It is these optimistic individuals who the employers regularly promote to leadership roles so that they bring about a new and enhanced approach within the organisation.

6. Reward Yourself

One of the key aspects of remaining motivated is to reward one's own performance. Employers, due to habit, only reward those actions which have a significant bearing on the performance of the organisation. They forget to reward the smaller victories that an individual achieves as, to most, they remain inconsequential to the larger schemes of things.

Change this; learn to reward yourself for your own achievements. It is even prudent that an individual must prepare a list of their personal and professional milestones. This list will serve both as a reminder as well as a 'to-do' list through which they can measure their individual success. When a milestone is achieved, give yourself a well-deserved reward. Remember: It's not about the size of either the achievement or the reward. It is all about recognising the hard work that you put into an important event, and your success is a consequence of your own abilities and talent.

In conclusion, individuals who wish to see themselves in a leadership role must spend time on improving their capabilities and strengths on a regular basis. In simple terms, before a leader or entrepreneur begins his journey to motivate others at the workplace, they must be highly self-motivated individuals themselves, only then will they be in a position to transfer this motivation to others within the organisation.

Motivating Employees at the Workplace

A workplace is a complex and constantly evolving environment. Successful entrepreneurs and business leaders are regularly moulding and shaping the organisational environment so as to create a viable working habitat in which they are able to motivate their employees to achieve the most beneficial result for the organisation. Let us discuss some important techniques to achieve such a practical workplace environment.

1. Orientation Programme on Joining the Organisation

One of the best practices followed by almost all Fortune 500 companies throughout the world is the organising of an orientation week for all the new employees who have recently joined them. This orientation week is considered to be an essential first step and is usually compulsory to attend. It is during that period of time when the new employees are indoctrinated with the value system of their new employer. This is also perhaps the first chance that both the employer and employee get to interact with each other on a real-time basis. Senior management takes this opportunity to hear for themselves the expectation of their newly inducted co-workers. Furthermore, they reinforce the values and tenets of the organisation so that the new employees have a clear understanding of the core beliefs of their new organisation as well as its hierarchy and, most importantly, the various systems in place which are there to help them achieve their best for the success of the organisation. Such orientation programmes play an integral part in motivating the average individual and affirming to them that they are in a progressive and fair organisation.

2. Mentorship Programme

It is but natural for a new employee within an organisation to feel nervous and intimidated with their new job role. This is a normal reaction for a large number of individuals who join a new organisation at various stages of their professional life. Organisations can implement certain programmes which can go a long way in alleviating such stress and anxiety. One such method is the introduction of a mentorship programme within the organisation. In programmes such as these, each new employee is partnered with an experienced co-worker who acts as their mentor. The mentor is tasked with the duty to make the new employee familiar with the working style within the organisation. They serve as both guide and counsellor and make sure that the employee has all the tools which may allow them to perform to the best of their abilities at their disposal. These mentorship programmes are usually only for a few days but play an effective role in the motivation of the new employee.

3. Give the Employees Purpose

It is important for every entrepreneur and business leader to share their vision with their employees. It is an effective practice for each employee to know, as far as possible, where they fit into the grand scheme of the organisation and, better still, to know how the work they are doing contributes to this vision. The knowledge that their contribution plays an important part in the future success of the organisation will most definitely motivate them to perform to the best of their abilities.

Furthermore, it also will propagate a sense of belonging and, more importantly, provide the employees with a renewed sense of purpose in going about their day to day activities.

4. Present a Clear Career Path

Most individuals join an organisation with a clear career goal. These career goals are special as well as unique to each individual. In simple terms, each person is motivated by the opportunity to achieve his personal goal. Employers must take out the time to discuss and carefully coordinate the best utilisation of that personal goal. To this effect, it is common to find employers who jointly create a well-defined career path for the individual employee. It serves two major purposes: The first is that it assures an employee that they are part of an organisation which has their best interests in mind, and secondly, the organisation benefits through an increase in the level of commitment and loyalty from their employees. Such systems, when placed correctly within an organisation, allow for mutually assured growth and success for the entire organisation.

5. Encourage Healthy Competition

Most entrepreneurs and business leaders are aware that a competitive environment is a productive environment. Many times, it is a common practice to arrange competitions and challenges within an organisation. The purpose of these competitions is to promote positive and constructive interaction between the employees. Such interactions foster unity between not only the employees but, more importantly, within the different departments within the organisation. Furthermore, the healthy competition allows employers to judge and compare the performance levels of each individual employee. Therefore, they are able to identify future potential leaders for the organisation. The converse is also true; the same process allows them to identify potential weakness in their employees, which can or may be rectified through advance training and guidance.

6. Effective Communication

Effective communication helps foster a robust working relationship between all levels within an organisation. It plays an integral part in improving efficiency and confidence within the different individuals engaged in various functions throughout the organisation. Effective communication is a two-way street. It allows for better alignment between the objectives of the organisation and the expectations of the employees. To put it simply, effective communication promotes a positive business environment by breaking down barriers and allows an organisation to overcome obstacles formed through culture, persona and experience. Effective communication allows an organisation to cultivate and encourage talent in line with the goals of the organisation. Furthermore, it improves the cohesion between co-workers and provides a more satisfying and diverse working environment for the employees. Any organisation which wishes to create an effective balance must adopt and firmly establish a culture of good communication within their organisation.

7. Let Them Lead

Every organisation's survival depends to a certain extent on its ability to identify and promote new leaders within it. Furthermore, such is the nature of business that it also provides enough opportunity for these leaders to be tested on a regular basis. It is irrelevant whether the opportunity or occasion is small or large. One of the most effective methods of encouraging employees is by putting them in a leadership role. This has many benefits; the most important are, first, it allows an organisation to review the performance of the individual selected for future assignments and leadership roles. Secondly and perhaps more importantly, each organisation has certain undeserving individuals who believe they are leadership material. Therefore, these individuals regularly push the management to promote them as leaders. It is most prudent to give individuals such as them an opportunity: If they perform successfully, the management will have discovered a new leader who had been overlooked. And if their performance does not inspire confidence, the management will always be able to motivate them to move on to other more suitable job roles. In both cases, the management has done its duty to motivate its employees. Therefore, each employee should be given at least one opportunity in the role of a leader.

8. Encourage Transparency

A high level of transparency within an organisation is an essential criterion for its success. Transparency within the workplace encourages the growth of trust and credibility between all levels of an organisation. It is important to give key employees regular insights into the functioning of a business organisation. This allows these key individuals to act as a regular feedback system, which, in turn, allows the top management to address all significant and urgent issues in a well-planned and coordinated effort. This being said, it is important to be careful with the kind of information as well as with who such information is shared.

Transparency within an organisation also means being fair and treating all employees in an equal manner. It implies that all members of the organisation must be treated with respect as well as be given equal opportunity to showcase their talents and ideas. A transparent work environment encourages an atmosphere of trust, confidence and hope within the individuals of an organisation to work as a team. It further translates into a positive belief in the vision of its leaders and the mission of the organisation. Therefore, in a workplace where individuals trust and repose faith in the actions of its leaders, the employees will always be highly motivated.

9. Provide Education and Professional Development

Most forward-thinking organisations realise that there is a great benefit which can be gained through providing their employees with the prospect of self-growth through offering relevant educational and professional development opportunities. Providing relevant and precise education and training is an essential investment in the future growth of an organisation. By providing such opportunities, the organisation sends a clear message to its employees: the organisation values their contribution and is more than willing to empower them for their future betterment. Furthermore, it allows the organisation to retain its top employees as well attract other top individuals from the business environment in which they operate.

In fact, it is a good practice to allocate sufficient funds to formalise employee education and development. This allows employees to realise that learning and growth should form an integral part of their belief and culture while they are a part of the organisation. A simple method is to introduce the prospect of forums of guidance where discussions about an employee's job role and future career paths can be debated, agreed and acted upon. Such a forum can easily provide the missing tools and education to help the employees achieve their fullest potential.

10. Recognise and Incentivise Employees Achievements

It is important to introduce a system which recognises and rewards the achievement of an employee within an organisation. The system must be able to do three things: First, identify the correct and deserving employee. Second, be able to measure the quantum of the effort and, lastly, provide an appropriate reward befitting the performance. It is not about only the act of recognition but, more importantly, the principle of rewarding those who go above and beyond the established standard.

The size of the recognition or incentive is not important, but it must be both valuable and desirable to the employees. It can be as simple as a compliment or even a reward which is financial in nature. It is common to find many types of incentive reward programmes within the same organisation. While some will reward individual performance, others will reward a team effort. In almost all cases, these incentives and rewards are a direct attempt to motivate the employees to produce their best performance on a regular basis. If an organisation is able to highlight the inherent value of a good performance to their employees, they shall always be successful in motivating them to keep growing and developing at the workplace.

Motivational Challenges

Workplace Conflict

One of the greatest challenges to motivating employees is having unresolved conflict in the workplace It is the attempt of every organisation to create a work environment which is conducive to the growth of the organisation. Certain instances which must be avoided at all costs are:

a. Open Disagreement with a Colleague

When any disagreement happens, it is a good practice for the senior staff members to invite the disagreeing parties to a closed room and give them an opportunity to resolve the matter amicably between them. If the matter is not resolved, only then should the senior manager step in and use his or her influence to resolve the matter.

b. Gossip and Personal Attacks

Rumour or misinformation is one of the greatest challenges in the modern workplace. There will always be some who will be mongers of gossip and will also indulge in attacking the sentiments of other workers. It is the duty of the senior management to identify those individuals and issue them a strict formal warning. In fact, in cases where the warning does not have the desired effect, the individual should be encouraged to seek professional help. If all else fails, it is best that the individuals are asked to leave the organisation.

1. Diverse and Cross-Cultural Workforce

An organisation is a meeting place of different-minded individuals, each with their well-defined personalities. It is the ability to manage this diversity which is the real challenge for the organisation. A simple example of this is the evident difference of age median which exists in almost all organisations around the world. The senior employees within the organisation prefer working in a highly structured method, while the younger members will consistently push for independent self-sufficiency and will be more open to trying new methods which can be implemented throughout the organisation.

Many organisations today are also spread across different geographical locations all around the world. There is a lot of cross-cultural exchange which takes place within the organisation. Individuals of different countries will most definitely work and behave in a method contradictory and opposing to their counterparts from other regions of the world. The true challenge for the organisation is to identify and introduce a method of open communication, where each counterpart is able to gain from the strengths and experiences of the others.

2. Appropriate Rewards and Recognition

As earlier acknowledged, it is important to reward and recognise both individual and team efforts within the organisation. The area in which most organisations fail or are found to be inconsistent is the correct amount and type of reward and recognition. In most cases, organisations fail to clearly define the parameters at which the reward and recognition become available to the individual or team. This failure to define those set parameters leads to employees overestimating the worth of their performance, and therefore, they are disappointed when they neither receive the level of reward nor the recognition they have built up themselves to receive. Therefore, it is the duty of the organisation to introduce a reward and recognition system which is consistent in its performance evaluation of all its employees. And the same system should be clearly communicated throughout the organisation.

3. Retaining the Top-Performing Employees

One of the greatest challenges of an organisation is to retain its top performers. It is a reality that there will be employees who will leave the organisation for better opportunities. Furthermore, such is the reality that rival organisations will attempt to poach the best performing employees of the organisation. Therefore, it is to the advantage of an organisation to adopt a proactive approach in offering appropriate rewards to their top-performing employees. Every effort should be made to enumerate the advantages of the current organisation as well as discuss the disadvantages that such a move would cause to the career path of the specific employee. However, in some cases, even after the best efforts, there will be individuals who may still leave the organisation for a better opportunity elsewhere. It is best to let such employees leave and hire or promote other individuals who can replace them.

In retrospection, all entrepreneurs are aware that no one is irreplaceable for the organisation. While at first the loss of some employees may seem to be serious, experience has shown that such setbacks are temporary in nature and such events allow most organisations to recover even stronger than before.

McClelland's Need Theory

With the advent of the modern organisation, the workplace became a melting point of social and cultural differences. Many great thinkers and academicians alike sensed the need to study and understand this new phenomenon. In most cases, they were intrigued by the human aspect of an organisation. Many thinkers have set out to answer the most important of all questions: "What motivates people at the workplace?" This line of study has allowed the discovery of various approaches and theories on this subject. One of the most relevant motivation theories in the present scenarios and, in my personal opinion, one of great importance to entrepreneurs and business leaders is McClelland's Need Theory.

It was around the year 1960 that David McClelland, an American psychologist, introduced his Three Needs Theory. McClelland pointed out that regardless of a person's age, sex and culture, each individual's life revolves around three basic aspects. These aspects and needs as identified by him were **achievement**, **power** and **affiliation**. He surmised that all individuals are in possession of at least one of these needs, and they are driven by it. He further elaborated that the need and requirement of individuals do not remain static, but in fact, they regularly change with the passage of time. Therefore, the way a person behaves at his workplace is directly influenced by the change in their personal environment. If the top management of an organisation is able to identify these motivational changes, they will be in a position to motivate the individual to put in their best effort to achieve the goals of the organisation.

Need for Achievement

As the name suggests, individuals who fall into this category are driven by the need for achieving. They are found to have a great ability to measure the reward and risk ratio within any situation. They are most likely to be found avoiding either a low-risk or low reward situation and are unable to execute a high risk and high reward situation at the workplace.

The reason for such a selection is that a low-risk reward does not challenge these individuals. And in situations which are high risk and high reward, they firmly believe that more than the effort that they put in, the result or the outcome is based less on their performance and more on luck and providence.

Individuals in this category are extremely result-oriented and are able to find a creative solution to even the most difficult situations. They crave feedback on all their workplace performance and treat it as an opportunity to further improve their performance for their organisation. They are regularly found to set a benchmark for themselves and their organisation, and in most cases, they consider achieving their personal goals as better rewards than financial ones. However, they are not very good team players and prefer to work by themselves. They are prone to being egoistic and sometimes give the impression that they are unapproachable and distant.

Need for Power

Individuals who belong to this category seek power and authority for themselves. They are driven by the single-minded goal of pursuing different avenues which would help them in acquiring influence at the workplace. They are motivated by competition, and they enjoy winning arguments. Their objective is to position themselves in a place of authority, where they can influence and convince their co-workers through their opinions and beliefs.

They make good leaders and team members. They are able to achieve this power through steady discipline and are able to persuade the same level of commitment from their team members. On the negative side, they are sometimes found making unwarranted compromises to win an argument or a contract. The only time they are able to accept losses is when, by doing so, it would lead to victory for their team and organisation. Therefore, it is precisely for this reason that individuals belonging to this category must be dealt with in a flexible yet firm manner. It is important to remember that while victory is a desirable outcome for any organisation, it should not come as a result of the loss of reputation or status. It is important that the organisation leaders set clear boundaries within which these individuals are allowed to operate and hold them accountable for the same.

Need for Affiliation

Individuals who belong to this category are most comfortable working in teams and in groups. They do not actively seek an opportunity to be put in a leadership role. They are content with maintaining fruitful relations within a team and strongly desire to be loved and accepted by their teammates. Individuals who are motivated by affiliation are averse to taking risks, simply because of an irrational fear of rejection by their peers, and are usually found to be quite pleased to follow the orders and desires of their senior management.

Furthermore, individuals in this category value the feelings of others over and above their own. They are eager to conform to the wishes of those people whose friendship and stature they admire and value. However, the strength of these individuals lies in their ability to maintain special relationships for the organisation over a long period of time. Their choice of collaboration over competition makes them ideal candidates in areas where an organisation needs to have social interactions with the public in general. They are best suited for business areas such as client services and customer relations.

In conclusion, it is a fact that each new entrant joins an organisation with great passion and hopes to make a valuable contribution through their performance. It is the work conditions and the policies within the workplace which play a great part in keeping them continuously motivated over a long period of time. It, therefore, becomes imperative for entrepreneurs and business leaders alike to realise that they are responsible for continuously maintaining the motivation levels within their organisations. To this effect, the McClelland's Need Theory provides a comprehensive system to alter the method of motivation on a need-based system throughout all levels of the organisation.

Chapter Eleven

Be You-nique: The Personal Branding Directive

"To be a great champion you must believe you are the best. If you're not, pretend you are."

Muhammad Ali
(American Professional Boxer and Activist)

The subject of personal branding is often considered by many to be part of brand creation of a business. This is true but only to a certain extent. Personal branding has very little to do with the brand of an organisation or business. Personal branding is where the individual becomes a brand which is separate and unique from their professional life. Furthermore, creating a strong personal brand, in many ways, helps in promoting the business as well. This is because a successful entrepreneur and business leader cannot be totally separate from the organisation they are part of.

In addition, given the level of competition existing in the global business environment, it has become increasingly important to utilise self-branding as an effective method of supporting the growth of a business. The new-age entrepreneur or business leader is well aware that the creation of a strong personal brand is essential to transmit the values, ideals and attributes that are representative of their own core beliefs. It is imperative to understand the intricacy and complexity which go hand in hand in creating a pragmatic personal brand.

Richard 'Virgin' Branson

Sir Richard Branson is a British business tycoon. He is the founder of the Virgin Group of companies, which has a stake or controlling interest in over 400 companies around the world. He is estimated to have a net worth of 5.1 billion pounds sterling.

Richard Branson is regarded by many as the poster boy of self-branding. His personal brand is estimated to be worth over 100 times his net worth. What sets him apart from other entrepreneurs and business leaders are the **unique stunts and showmanship** he employs to promote his businesses. To illustrate this special talent, I have presented three real-life examples of his distinctive style of personal branding—a personal style which not only promotes the product he is selling but simultaneously also enhances his own personal brand.

Illustration 1: Virgin Atlantic

In the year 2007, when Virgin Atlantic Airline launched its first flight between San Francisco and Las Vegas, Richard Branson developed a stunt which saw him jump off the 407 feet high Palms Hotel Casino in Las Vegas, attached to nothing more than a bungee rope. However, due to the presence of strong gusty winds, the stunt did not go as originally planned. Richard Branson twice hit the side of the building and literally ripped his pants before he landed safely on the ground.

While any other individual would have been shaken and would have retired after such an incident, Richard Branson attended a press conference and even joked about how badly the stunt had gone off. It is important here to realise that even though his body, as well as his ego, had taken a beating that day, Richard Branson chose to take the incident in his stride and turn it into a spectacle, which then allowed him to monopolise the incident to promote not only his airline but also to enhance his own personal brand image of being a bold, courageous and fearless entrepreneur.

Illustration 2: The Cross-Dressed Flight Attendant

This incident took place in 2010. Richard Branson and Tony Fernandes, AirAsia CEO, are competitors in the airline business and they own their own Formula 1 Grand Prix racing teams. It is believed that Tony Fernandes bet Richard Branson that his team 'Lotus' would finish the racing season ahead of the 'Virgin Racing' team, to which Richard Branson quipped that if that were to happen, then Richard Branson would dress up as a female air hostess for AirAsia. As it came to be, Lotus did finish the racing season ahead of Virgin Racing.

The man that Richard Branson is, he did exactly as he had promised; he not only donned an air hostess uniform but further went on to wax his legs and completed his look with the application of makeup. Furthermore, he even served Tony Fernandes coffee on the flight or, more precisely, deliberately spilt the coffee on the AirAsia boss's lap. The question most frequently raised about this incident is this: Who exactly gained mileage through this unique occasion, the AirAsia Group or Richard Branson and his Virgin Group?

Richard Branson later revealed that the air hostess stunt had accumulated over $300,000 for the Starlight Foundation, an organisation which supports terminally ill children and is regularly supported by both AirAsia and Virgin Airlines—proving that behind that business mind also exists a man with a golden heart.

Illustration 3: The Launch of Virgin Cola in the United States

In 1998, Richard Branson launched his own brand of cola, wickedly named Virgin Cola, in the United States of America. During this time, Coca Cola and Pepsi Cola were the global leaders in the market. Richard Branson was well aware that creating space in this business would be a difficult task. It was a hard task because till that time, no other company had even attempted a direct 'Cola War' with the two global giants, that too in their own backyard.

Richard Branson and his team knew that they needed to come up with a spectacular event which would both shock as well as garner the maximum publicity for the maiden launch of Virgin Cola. So, Richard Branson chose to ride down Fifth Avenue in a military tank and proceeded to blow up a Coca Cola sign right at the centre of Times Square in New York. This marketing marvel was captured and beamed across the world by various news channels, and for a small period of time, it captured the attention of people throughout the world.

However, in the end, Virgin Cola was not able to live up to that initial publicity, and its sales plummeted after some time. In fact, Virgin Cola today is retailed only in a few areas within the United Kingdom and a few Asian and European markets. It, till date, accounts as one of the biggest failures for Richard Branson and his company.

What is significant to note is that Richard Branson has continually associated his self-brand with that of his company such that these two separate brands are synonymous with each other. This co-existence is not by chance or by accident; it is a well thought out marketing strategy which promotes the ideology that any business is a reflection of its owners and promoters. Therefore, it is important to realise that the Virgin Group is a reflection of the philosophies, beliefs and principals of its founder, Richard Branson. It is these attributes which have given recognition to the organisation and allowed it to become a separate brand by its own right. It should then come as no surprise that it is Richard Branson who is the true brand of the Virgin Group and not the other way around.

The Benefits of Building a Personal Brand

Self-Discovery

One of the most important benefits of building a personal brand is that to create it, the entrepreneur and business leader must first reflect and identify those attributes that make them special and unique. These attributes must be tangible aspects of their own personality and must be a marketable characteristic. In most cases, this journey of self-discovery serves two distinctive and important functions. It allows individuals to evaluate themselves and discover those attributes, both positive and negative, which are an integral part of their mental persona and, more importantly, are known privately to them only.

The other important aspect is that in some cases, the individuals discover that they do not possess any such tangible, marketable or distinctive quality. Thus, this discovery either causes them to give up on their desire of building their personal brand or, as in most cases, these individuals begin to step out of their comfort zone and set about changing and developing themselves so as to acquire those positive attributes which would be instrumental in projecting them as unique and exceptional individuals in the near future.

Improves Communication Skills

Personal branding is, above all, about communicating a relevant message to a targeted audience. To this effect, the main objective of communication is threefold: the message generated must be clear, simple and transferred in its entirety from start to finish. It is important to realise that the message is an attempt by the sender to generate a response from the receiver of the said communication. In fact, any communication, both within an organisation as well as external communication, must be structured in a precise and well-formulated format so that it is understood and comprehensible to a large section of the employees as well as the public in general. It, therefore, is paramount to reflect on the words utilised within the communication so as to send a powerful and genuine message. Furthermore, to build a successful personal brand, the individual must present his message in a way which persuades his audience to share his confidence and conviction in the subject matter being conveyed. Therefore, the prerequisite of building a successful personal brand needs an individual to regularly dedicate both time and effort in improving one's own communication skills.

Builds Relationship with the Target Audience

It is essential to realise that your message must reach the right people, which does not necessarily mean the whole world. The success of a personal brand depends greatly on communicating the proper message to the correct target audience. It is important to identify that target audience with which an emotional connection can be forged. Therefore, to create a successful brand, you will have to invest time and effort in building a credible and trustworthy relationship with your target audience. The most successful entrepreneurs and business leaders are aware that in the real world, the opinions of other people matter. People tend to be more comfortable doing business with those who they have heard about from trustworthy and authentic sources.

Therefore, by creating an emotional connection with a target audience, the entrepreneur and business leader are, in fact, building their own team of influencers, who, in turn, will be in a position to influence others on the positive aspects and attributes of doing business with the individual associated with that personal brand. In fact, the target audience becomes a de facto marketing team for that personal brand. Hence, both time and effort must be spent to build a viable and long-lasting relationship with your audience such that they themselves begin to believe that they are also important associates and stakeholders who are engaged in the well-being of your professional journey.

Builds Authenticity

A personal brand is a reflection of the true nature of the individual it represents. Your personal brand should elaborate your attributes and strengths and, at the same time, deflect the attention away from your inherent weaknesses. It is essential to never fake your brand. In many cases, individuals get influenced by reading and observing other individuals and begin to copy them. However, by adopting this copy and paste attitude, they set up their personal brands for failure even before getting started.

The essence of authenticity is to promote those attributes which do not get an opportunity to reveal themselves due to an individual's association with their organisation. This authenticity is that part which is personal and special to the mental make up of each and every person. A personal brand should always be an expression of those hidden talents and elements which define us. The creation of a personal brand should be treated as an opportunity to declare to the world that **'This is who I am... Unbiased and Unashamed'**. And finally, a personal brand does not seek acceptance, nor is it a competition; far from that, in fact, it represents the prospect of self-discovery and freedom from judgement.

Builds Credibility

Building a personal brand allows entrepreneurs and business leaders to enhance their reputation in the world of business. It allows them to promote themselves as champions of change as well as influencers of public thought and opinion. To this effect, they strive to create a lasting impression in the minds of others by spending a great deal of time in promoting their own thought philosophy. To reach the largest audience possible, it is also imperative to utilise all avenues of promotion. While there are many who would support the traditional avenues of promotion, the new-age leader is a master of promotion through social media. The objective is to increase their reach to the public, and without a doubt, it is social media which provides them with an appropriate avenue.

Building credibility is all about continuously and consistently transmitting the same message again and again to a target audience. The more clear and trustworthy the information being transmitted, the more chances of it appealing to a newer audience. Therefore, requisite time and effort must be taken to first investigate and scrutinise the genuineness of the information being used to garner support for personal branding so that it will be more successful in the long run. Eventually, a personal brand must be a true representation of the individual and the organisation it promotes. A false promotion may increase the popularity in the short term, but if the brand is an attempt at false or artificial depiction, it will never be able to gain a true sense of credibility or trustworthiness within its target audience.

Creates Focus

Personal branding is about establishing an individual's name as an expert in their area of a specific and tangible speciality. However, many individuals make the mistake of presenting themselves as experts in many other fields. This attempt causes them to lose focus on their core endowment or main talent. This lack of focus on a specific and well-defined speciality deems them to fail even before they have started. It is, therefore, essential to be clear about the various attributes that define you as a unique individual. Once those traits and qualities are identified, then it is time to set about amplifying them to the most appropriate audience using the most suitable medium at their disposal. The importance of focus defines the type of message which would eventually be produced and transmitted. It is focus which would allow an individual to attain the best return on the time invested in promoting their personal brand. And it will be focus which allows entrepreneurs and business leaders to take control of their careers and professional growth trajectory.

Makes You more Resourceful

Entrepreneurs and business leaders are aware that almost all resources are finite in nature; that is, eventually, with the passage of time, they will diminish and come to an end. It is, therefore, essential to utilise the best resources at one's disposal. In most cases, resources are limited due to their cost and by the period they are available. The challenge in building a personal brand is in identifying the most appropriate medium and forum to present one's opinion to the largest target audience. Both the medium and forum will be restricted by the money and time available at the disposal of the individual to whom the personal brand belongs. Therefore, it is of great importance to inculcate a convention of carefully selecting and choosing those options which would allow the maximum exposure with the least burden on the finances and constraints of time.

Certain techniques employed by the best personal brands are co-branding and co-sharing of resources. This allows other like-minded personal brands to create a network which allows each individual to gain promotion at a fraction of the cost as well as allows for regular and constant promotion for a longer period of time.

Techniques for Building a Personal Brand

Create Your Vision

A personal brand should be treated as a personal vision statement. Any vision statement is by default unique in nature. Its boundaries are limited by the individuals who create them. Therefore, you and only you are the master of your personal brand. It is essential to be absolutely clear when identifying the relevant qualities of any personal brand. As discussed earlier, each individual may possess many positive characteristics. However, when it comes to building a personal brand, only the most dominant virtues or traits should form the core of the personal brand. And only those main qualities should be shared and propagated to the public. Therefore, each individual must spend quality time in selecting those traits which may enhance their intrinsic value and only then proceed to broadcast them to the general public.

Define Your Audience

The term 'general public' includes each and every person who has access to your personal brand and, therefore, has the ability to either appreciate or criticise the persona you share with the world. Your 'target audience' are those persons who you would like to choose and, therefore, influence their thoughts and actions. Your target audience has a special existence and stands apart from the general public. Therefore, any individual who wishes to create a successful personal brand must first identify which strata or group they wish to convert from the general public into their target audience.

It is essential to first specifically and carefully define what type of audience you wish to interact with. To get started, you may define your audience on the basis of age, gender, occupation or even marital status. Whatever trait, attribute or characteristic you choose, it must be explicit, precise and permanent, simply because a personal brand's success depends, to a great extent, on the message or information it shares with its audience. The more consistent and reliable the message remains over a long period of time, the more the probability of the personal brand achieving greater heights of success.

Build Your Online Presence

Nearly everyone today uses social networking sites like Facebook, Instagram, Twitter and many more. Therefore, there should be no doubt about the benefits that a personal brand may acquire by using such platforms for their promotion. In today's day and age, social media is a powerful instrument in sharing and transmitting information to all corners of the world.

To this effect, it is important for individuals who wish to promote their personal brand through social media to improve their participation and become more active members of different online communities. Special emphasis should be given to creating relevant content that would allow your followers to share and repost the same message in other communities. This sharing and interaction will play a great part in gaining and enhancing your reputation as well as allow you to garner a new and undiscovered audience.

Build Your Offline Presence

While many individuals may believe that the use of social media to promote a personal brand is a good idea, many will also like to promote their personal brand through other means such as traditional marketing. Traditional marketing or offline promotion encompasses marketing through billboards, newspapers, flyers as well as television commercials and radio spots. It is important to realise that traditional marketing has a far more proven record of success as compared to social marketing or offline marketing. Therefore, it is always a good idea to utilise a marketing plan which is a combination of both. By doing this, a personal brand would be able to maximise its reach potential and cover a larger section of their target audience. Furthermore, it would allow for the creation of a more cost-effective and better marketing mix for the personal brand.

Build Your Network of Cooperation

One of the most overlooked aspects of building a personal brand is the advantages which can be gained through network cooperation. That is to say, there are always individuals and companies alike who seek to be associated with other meaningful brands. Therefore, there will always be opportunities for co-branding and product placements, which would be beneficial to both the parties concerned.

Network cooperation increases a personal brand's exposure to a newer audience and, therefore, can play an important role in increasing its reach and influence. It is no secret that the larger your network becomes, the greater the chances of newer avenues and opportunities for brand promotion. Therefore, it is always a good practice to gracefully accept it when presented with such opportunities, and the same should be utilised to its fullest potential.

Control Your Content

The value of your personal brand is directly proportional to the content you share with your audience. It is important to realise that you control all aspects of your personal brand. By adopting a systematic control over the content, you will directly be in a position to control the perception of your personal brand. Therefore, before you post, upload or share any material, it will be prudent to consider all the potential effects that the content you share will have on your personal brand in the long term. The public space, whether it be a social network or the real world, is not a forgiving space, and public perception is very fickle in nature. Therefore, only your content will decide what your brand will eventually become. That being the case, it is essential to be cautious and verify all aspects relating to the content before it is shared in the public domain.

Invite Feedback and Evolve

Many personal brands do not invite any sort of feedback from their target audience. Due to this habit, they lose out on an opportunity to interact with the very people who they wish to influence. It is important to realise that not all the content shared by the personal brand will be appreciated at face value. It is normal for some within the target audience to feel offended or even detached from the content being transmitted. The direct effect of such a situation is that the personal brand will begin to lose a number of its regular followers and, in extreme cases, may even stagnate and eventually cease to exist.

Therefore, it is to the advantage of the personal brand to encourage its audience to send it feedback and share their opinions and suggestions with the promoters of the personal brand. By encouraging feedback from the audience it serves, the personal brand will be in a position to quickly gauge the changing trends and choices in the public domain. This, in turn, would allow the personal brand to become proactive and allow it the opportunity to adapt and evolve faster to the needs and desires of its target audience.

Conclusion

In conclusion, one of the most important ingredients in building a personal brand is having fun in the process. Building a personal brand is more about the journey. Building a personal brand is about discovering yourself and the world around you. By far, it is one of the best learning experiences that anyone can go through. In the end, your personal brand is an expression of your self and your opinion and personal beliefs. Therefore, have fun discovering yourself and enjoy the expedition!

Goffman's Self-Presentation Theory

The advent of personal branding is a recent phenomenon. Hence, there is no clear-cut concept or theory which has either been presented or accepted by the great thinkers and theorists of our time. However, I would like to introduce the reader to a very interesting theory which was introduced by Erwin Goffman in the year 1959 in a book titled 'The Presentation of Self in Everyday Life'.

Goffman presented a theory which was based on the hypothesis that all individuals are actors in real life and play different roles and react differently to different situations during the same day; for example, the way an individual acts differently while speaking to a parent, a child, a boss or his office co-workers. He introduced the Dramaturgy Approach and through this approach developed and introduced many concepts, which, in turn, revolutionised the subject of micro-sociology. His concept of Self-Presentation Theory can be broadly classified into three clear and distinctive zones.

On Stage Zone

The 'On Stage Zone' is similar to an individual who is the lead actor in a play. All aspects such as dialogue, lighting as well as the performance of other actors are choreographed in such a way that the main lead is presented to be larger than life. This is similar to the attributes utilised by individuals who attempt to promote their self-branding. These individuals will always present and promote their best qualities as well as hide and conceal their bad attributes and weaknesses.

It is important here to realise that whatever is communicated by a self-brand is tightly controlled and created to be transmitted to a specific target audience. Therefore, it is prudent to verify all assertions and claims of any personal brand before following or promoting it, lest they prove to be false.

Off Stage Zone

The 'Off Stage Zone' is also referred to as the 'backstage'. It is that zone where an individual can be their true selves, without any pretence or façade. In the context of self-branding, it is that zone which most individuals will try and conceal from their target audience. It is a place where the individuals are confident that they will not be judged or scrutinised on account of their performance. It is a zone where individuals can afford to let down their guard and reveal their true nature, which may also expose their true human frailties and shortcomings. To put it simply, the 'Off Stage Zone' is the complete opposite of and separate from the 'On Stage Zone'. It is a private zone, much the same as a safe house where none of an individual's target audience exists, and nor can they enter without the expressed desire of the individual concerned.

Zone of Transition

The 'Zone of Transition' is that area which exists in between as well as outside the 'On Stage Zone' and 'Off Stage Zone'. It is that zone which is the middle or grey zone; it is that area where all things are in suspension or at rest. That is to say, there exists a situation where the individuals are neither required to impress or propagate their good attributes as well as hide or conceal their true frailties or shortcomings.

In the true sense, the zone between the stage world and the real world is disconnected. To put it simply, all individuals are located in this zone, and that is in the 'Zone of Transition'. As and when different situations and circumstances present themselves, the individuals must decide which zone is the most appropriate for them and then initiate action accordingly. In fact, Erwin Goffman identified the 'Zone of Transition' as the most important and interesting area of study in his entire theory of dramaturgy.

Chapter Twelve

Viable Succession Plan

"Before you are a leader,
Success is all about growing yourself.
When you become a leader,
Success is all about growing others."

Jack Welch
(Chairman and CEO, General Electric 1981-2001)

One of the most uncomfortable and harsh realities known to entrepreneurs and business leaders alike is that there will come a time when they will have to retire or step down from the company they helped set up. To this effect, it is one of their greatest endeavours to put in place individuals who will continue in their place and secure the future of the organisation. Therefore, many leaders will take proactive steps and put in place a viable succession plan within the organisation well in advance of that eventuality.

Setting up a viable succession plan is by far one of the most overlooked processes in a business organisation. It is one of the most important components for the well-being of an organisation which wishes to continue and grow in the future. A succession plan is found to be most useful in addressing those issues which arise when individuals in key positions retire, resign or have their services terminated. A viable succession plan put in place allows for a smooth transition by already having in place a readymade group of individuals to replace those holding key positions within the organisation. In fact, if planned with due diligence and with sufficient time, it becomes an exceedingly manageable event. In simple terms, a succession plan is a strategy to identify, educate and retain those individuals who demonstrate the most potential of becoming leaders in the future.

Illustration: Replacing Steve Jobs

Steve Jobs, the iconic founder of Apple, stepped down as the chief executive officer of the company he had created on August 24, 2011. As most industry experts were aware, Steve Jobs had been diagnosed with pancreatic cancer, and while at first, it did seem he would make a recovery, that sadly was not the case. Steve Jobs' passion and dedication to his organisation were never in doubt, as he tirelessly worked to make Apple one of the largest and most successful organisations of the world.

Many would agree that Steve Jobs was a visionary and was well aware of the importance of putting in place a viable succession plan. To this effect, he had already selected Tim Cook as a potential future replacement for himself as the next CEO of Apple. Steve Jobs was very clear that he would choose his successor from within the organisation. He was of the strong opinion that it is better to choose a successor who was well aware of and familiar with Apple's way of doing things. Therefore, it came as no surprise that he selected Tim Cook, who had held the reins of the organisation twice—in 2004 and then again in 2009—both the times Steve Jobs was unavailable due to his health issues.

Furthermore, Steve Jobs himself formulated and designed a curriculum for Tim Cook which would allow his future successor to spend quality time in almost all the departments which were an integral part of the Apple organisation. Steve Jobs encouraged Tim Cook to further create his own team and regularly put them in difficult and complex decision-making situations. Therefore, when the time eventually came for Steve Jobs to step down, he had no hesitation in recommending Tim Cook to take his place. In his resignation letter, he clearly stated, **"As far as my successor goes, I strongly recommend that we execute our succession plan and name Tim Cook as CEO of Apple."**

Thus, it came to be that Tim Cook replaced Steve Job as the CEO of Apple. Since Tim Cook took over in 2011, Apple has gone from strength to strength and is well on its way to becoming a trillion-dollar company. On Thursday 2nd August 2018, the share price of Apple hit $207.05 on the NASDAQ, and Apple became the first publically traded tech giant to reach the much-coveted $1 trillion market capitalisation in the United States.

In conclusion, it is important to realise that the continuity of an organisation is always the paramount concern to entrepreneurs and business leaders alike. To this effect, each organisation must spend quality time and effort in creating and implementing a viable and practical succession plan which can be put into operation as and when the situation arises in the future. Therefore, it is important to realise the benefits of creating a succession plan in the first place.

Benefits of Creating a Succession Plan

Most entrepreneurs and business leaders are aware of the importance of inducting a viable succession plan within their organisation. However, most are not aware of the many benefits of having such a succession plan put in place. There are many benefits of creating a viable succession plan within an organisation. Some of the most important benefits are discussed below.

A Proactive Approach

The very act of putting in place a succession plan signifies that the top management is conscious of their duty to safeguard the future of all stakeholders within their organisation. This move is suggestive of proactive entrepreneurs and business leaders who believe in securing the future of their organisation in the advent of some unforeseen event. It is usually put in place for those times when a situation may arise in which the current leadership, due to any **unanticipated reason,** is not at the helm of affairs. The objective is that the organisation must survive and grow at all possible costs. In most cases, it is a **reserve emergency plan**, where each of the important posts within an organisation has a backup replacement in place. The effort of a succession plan is to protect the organisation from a leadership vacuum. Therefore, putting in place a viable succession plan allows the organisation to be prepared for all future contingencies as and when they may occur.

Benefit of Introspection

One of the greatest benefits of creating a succession plan is the advantage it offers: an opportunity to introspect about the hierarchal system within an organisation. To this effect, most organisations employ a SWOT (Strengths, Weaknesses, Opportunities and Threats) analysis system of their current management matrix. This allows the top management to evaluate and investigate all possible combinations and arrangements which are possible so as to create a viable backup plan for the future of the organisation. This introspection allows for some crucial and decisive decisions to be taken so as to improve the efficiency of the organisation in the present. Furthermore, and more importantly, it allows the organisation to take those essential steps which would secure the greatest possible continued existence of the organisation in the future.

Gap Analysis

Most organisations create posts and positions within their hierarchy system on two bases. These posts are either **need-based** or **time-based**. However, given the rise of technology and specialisation in the global business environment, many organisations feel comfortable giving more responsibility in the hands of a few key players. To this effect, a succession plan must be capable of identifying such crucial individuals within an organisation. This, in turn, allows the identification of the potential gaps which exist in the hierarchy of an organisation. These gaps, if not dealt with soon, have an undesirable effect on the stability of the organisation in the near short term. But more importantly, they may also affect the very survival of the organisation in the future.

Organisation Culture and Values

Every business leader and entrepreneur is well aware of the importance of the culture and values which they propagate within their organisations. The organisation's culture and core values play an essential part in the way the organisation is perceived by the people it employs and the customers it provides its services to. Any organisation, regardless of its number of employees and size, can benefit greatly from the culture and values it offers its employees on a day to day basis. An organisation where the employees are introduced to a morally upright culture and values will further improve the trust and beliefs between the employees and the owners. This, in turn, will allow an environment to be created which is both progressive and conducive to the successful growth of the business and organisation in the long run.

Benefit of Discovering Future Leaders

Discovering future leaders within the organisation is one of the key responsibilities of a business leader and entrepreneur. Each organisation is made up of employees from different backgrounds, ideologies and a unique skill set which enriches the talent pool available in order to identify the new leaders of the future. Discovering and identifying potential future leaders early in their career allow the senior leadership an opportunity to train and inculcate the chosen few with tools and training so as to take the organisation to newer heights of success, securing the very future of the organisation they played an integral part in creating in the first place.

Benefit of Attracting and Retaining the Best Employees

The success and growth of any organisation are directly proportional to the quality of persons they employ. Organisations which are able to provide their employees with a clear path of self-development and other avenues of opportunities for valued advancement will, in the long term, attract persons of greater calibre and competence. Furthermore, when the same new employee attains a level of personal and professional satisfaction, they will continue within that same organisation for many productive years. Thus, it is important for organisations to frame and implement such programmes which will attract fresh candidates and will provide them with a strong rationale to remain committed to the organisation for the long term.

Succession Development

In the world of business, there are two methods which have been observed to be most acceptable to global organisations when they seek to resolve an issue with regard to succession development. These two methods are the **succession planning method** and the **replacement planning method**. Though both these methods seem relatively similar, they both lead to divergent results. Therefore, the need for understanding their separate characteristics is essential, as only then will we be in a position to implement them in the correct way and, in turn, reap their benefits.

The Succession Planning Method

The succession planning method is a long-term strategy. Its main objective is to develop the talent within an organisation so that as and when the vacancy arises, the same will be filled by the existing talent within the organisation itself. The succession planning method consists of five clear and distinctive stages. Each of these stages plays an important and integral part, and in most cases, they are co-dependent on each other. The main objective of the succession planning process is to provide a practical approach which would allow the organisation to consider all major aspects and issues which can influence or adversely affect the future continuity of the organisation.

Stage 1: Identifying Critical Posts Within the Organisation

In this stage, the organisation identifies those posts and positions which are essential and vital for the survival of the organisation. To identify these positions, the organisation will need to internally review each and every post and position that it offers to its employees. While it is true that this is a time-consuming procedure, it becomes the base and foundation for all future reduction and expansion of the workforce within an organisation.

Stage 2: Identifying the Capabilities and Competencies of the Workforce

In this stage, the organisation considers for itself what the key requirements or qualities are that an individual must possess to be in a position to fill up the critical post, should the need arise. The advantage of this stage is that it allows an organisation to distinguish the true nature of its workforce. Areas such as an individual's capability, potential, talent and aptitude are measured to a set criterion and kept in a record for future reference. Furthermore, it allows the organisation the chance to introduce various schemes to allow employees the benefit of learning and self-improvement, which then allows them to improve their performance within the organisation.

Stage 3: Identify the Potential Future Leaders and Their Abilities

The third stage is where the post within the hierarchy and the potential of the employees are compared and matched so as to identify the future potential leaders of the organisation. To this effect, the organisation is then able to build an effective pool of talent from which it can draw potential leaders as and when the situation arises in the future. It further allows the organisation to hold one-on-one discussions with the selected employees and work out a tailor-made growth plan for these individuals so that both they and the organisation are able to work out a mutually beneficial relationship and further strengthen their bonds of association.

Stage 4: Document and Implement Succession Plan

This stage perhaps is the most important in the succession planning method. It is a well-established fact that many organisations discuss the issue of succession planning. It is also true that they invest time and effort in identifying potential leaders. However, what all of them lack or fail to do is to process and record their findings into a proper structure or document which should be readily available to the decision-making hierarchy as and when the need for succession planning arises.

It is usually seen that in almost all cases, the entire succession planning process is lost, and the findings are never actually implemented. Therefore, it is essential to put in place a system which is able to safely implement the final and predetermined solutions of the succession planning process, only then will the entire process yield the best potential results for the organisation as a whole.

Stage 5: Review Effectiveness of Succession Plan

It is important to realise that a business organisation is always in a fluid state. That is to say, there are many factors, both internal as well as external, which change through the passage of time. In the same way, a succession plan is also privy to these changes. Therefore, it is in the larger interest of the organisation to continuously review and update the plan of succession at regular intervals of time.

Replacement Planning Method

The replacement planning method is a very specific and precise process. The objective of this method is to especially focus on the replacement of the top level of management within an organisation. Usually, this method is adopted for the top three positions in the organisational hierarchy, and it does not concern itself with the other lower levels within the organisation. It is a method which encourages an incumbent leader to select his future successor. To this effect, the selected individuals will be groomed over a long period of time before they eventually take their specific position of authority within the organisational hierarchy.

The replacement planning method has four clear and distinctive stages:

Stage 1: Initiation

In the initiation stage, an organisation usually will identify those individuals who show the most potential of becoming future leaders. It is a usual practice to hold orientation programmes for such individuals so as to make them aware of the organisation's core values and beliefs. These orientation programmes are specifically designed by the top leaders of the organisation and targeted to help locate their potential replacements at the earliest possible stage of an individual's career.

Stage 2: Selection

In the second stage, each top leader will then select two or three individuals who, in their opinion, show the greatest potential to replace them in the future. These potential replacements will then be put through a series of tests and examinations so as to identify their core competencies and potential weaknesses. These replacements will be tested both on an individual basis (against each other) as well as put together in various real-life business situations so as to identify a singular replacement candidate for the future. This process is extremely time-consuming and can span from a few months to a couple of years before the perfect replacement candidate is eventually selected.

Stage 3: Education or Training

The third stage begins once the specific replacement candidate is selected. In this stage, the selected candidate is put through an exhaustive process of education and training, all of which is custom-made and relative to the individual candidate and their job role. The ultimate objective of this stage is to prepare the candidate for all possible situations which may arise in the future. Furthermore, the hope is that when faced with that adversity, the potential candidate will resolve the situation, keeping intact the core values and beliefs which were inculcated within them at the very beginning of the replacement process, and is able to balance the aims and objectives of the organisation he serves and matches the trust and expectations of the leader who had selected him in the very first place.

Stage 4: Transition

The fourth and final stage is the transition stage. In this stage, the incumbent leader of the organisation hands over his authority to his chosen successor, and the chosen successor takes over the responsibility within the organisation in their designated leadership role.

In conclusion, there are many methods and processes which are available to business leaders and organisations throughout the globe. The above two methods presented continue to be the most preferred systems today. In the end, any method or process selected for succession planning is an individual and personal decision which should be carefully planned and formulated by the top leadership within the organisation.

Section 2

Gaurav Tekriwal

Vedic Maths Forum
Founder

Gaurav Tekriwal is the founder and president of Vedic Maths Forum India. He is one of the foremost authorities in the subject of Vedic Maths in the country. He is a well-established author of the Maths Sutra series of books. He has been featured in various television programmes and has been instrumental in introducing the Vedic Maths System to over 4 million students in India, South Africa, United States, Australia, UAE, Ghana, Colombia and New Zealand. He is a much sought-after speaker at public events and is a five-time TED/ TEDx speaker. Gaurav has been named one of India's Top Young Visionaries by the Ministry of External Affairs of India. He has most recently been recognised by the Honourable Governor of West Bengal for his contribution to the field of Vedic Mathematics.

1. Can you name a person who has had a tremendous impact on you as a leader? Why and how did this person impact your life?

One of my cousins had a tremendous impact on me when I was looking for a path to walk on. I was an equity research analyst in his company as an intern about 12 years ago, and he mentored me through his actions. He always asked me to follow one's passion and then success is bound to follow. He showed me the way on how to manage and grow a company. He showed me his vision and mission and exposed me to his company's continuous education programme, among many other things. He is an inspiration and a role model to me, as he made a difference in my life

2. What is one single characteristic that you believe every leader should possess?

That single characteristic is **focus**. In fact, this is one of the recurring topics which I share with the many people I interact with during my public engagements. If anyone is to succeed in any field, they must spend adequate time to train their minds to focus on the matter at hand.

3. What advice would you give someone going into a leadership position for the first time?

I would advise them to cultivate two distinct characteristics. The first is to 'Be Yourself'. While it is fine to be inspired by the actions of others, ultimately it is your originality of thoughts and actions which will allow you to succeed. The second is 'Understate and Over Deliver'. Many persons, in their enthusiasm, are prone to over-exaggeration, which eventually leads them to fail. It is best to take a guarded approach when promising results so that should they not be delivered, your respect and esteem are not diminished.

4. What's the most important leadership lesson you've learnt and how is it valuable?

Early on as a start-up, our organisation did not have any HR policies in place. One of the employees started taking advantage of the same and started discouraging our other employees from not only to coming to office but also started spreading rumours and indulging in misrepresentation and, further, indulged in office politics. When we found out, it was too late.

This was an important leadership lesson for me personally and taught me to properly introspect on where we had failed and what was needed to be done. To this effect, we introduced a well-prepared HR policy and then propagated the same throughout our entire organisation such that each employee had a clear understanding of the rules and regulations governing the working environment. We now strive to make the workplace positive with the help of these policies.

5. What accomplishment are you most proud of?

Representing India's heritage like Vedic Mathematics to global audiences as India's ambassador makes me feel proud.

6. What are you doing to ensure your continued growth and development as a leader?

I am myself on a continuous education programme ever since my graduation. It is in my nature to keep an open mind towards adopting new technologies for business efficiency, reading new books, organising talks and discussions on areas new to me and learning from others—these habits have kept me in good stead. Also, networking and getting to learn about new businesses have helped me develop myself as a leader. Furthermore, creating an environment in my company where learning never stops and where everyone strives to learn and practice courses as varied as Pranic Healing and even Digital Marketing.

7. As an individual who has a busy professional life, how would you say your family contributed to your success?

As a first-generation entrepreneur, I feel that my family has greatly contributed to my success. They have not only cushioned and incubated me from the failures early on in my career but also grounded me to stay humble in periods of success. My family is my support system, always encouraging me, whether that is in the middle of the night when I am writing books or even just before taking a critical business decision. In almost all decisions, their help and advice have been invaluable. I couldn't have achieved all that I have without them, and today I can proudly say that I built my career standing on the shoulders of titans—my family.

8. How do you keep your employees (or team members) keen and motivated?

Transparency is the key here, I feel. We lay down our policies for each department and, further, monitor the performance of our employees.

We ensure that rather than having individual goals, we have team goals, and the career path of each individual is clearly defined. Over and above, professionally we arrange for their learning and development so that they can add value to the company. We regularly meet for informal lunches and dinners so that team bonding takes place, and that in turn motivates them to put their best efforts.

9. Social media today is an effective medium of communication. It can make or break the reputation of an organisation as well as its leader. How would you advise a leader should approach the transmission of his or her organisation's brand over this medium?

You have rightly conveyed that social media can be a double-edged sword. So, we have professionals to manage it. We make a social media calendar at the beginning of each month, and we stick to the posts and schedule them beforehand. I feel social media is a great boon to spread the word about your business to a higher scale. Today we have only been able to scale up our business globally due to social media. The message of Vedic Maths is growing and so are our revenues. One should be honest and spread the right message about one's products and offerings and not just beat about the bush on social media. Doing this will cause people to look through you and can even force them to regard your brand as a fake.

10. What steps are taken within the organisation to discover new leadership within your organisation? How would you go about preparing the individual for his/her future role?

It's simple; if one is taking initiatives, you can see and feel the positive vibes. If someone is not, you will see their excuses for not doing a particular task. It is from within your existing team where you will find leaders. Leaders are not found overnight; you have to groom the fire inside them and then you will find team members who can take on critical responsibilities. You have to believe in them and show your faith in their abilities, and only when they realise their true potential will they shine bright like a diamond in your company as future leaders.

Prateek Jhajharia

Madhusudan Organics Ltd
Managing Director

Prateek Jhajharia is a young and dynamic leader and currently holds the position of managing director of Madhusudan Organics Ltd. He has held this position since 2008, and his sheer perseverance and hard work have allowed him to be recognised as one of the potential new age leaders in his field of operation. Prateek holds a Post Graduate Diploma in Finance from ICFAI and has been awarded a Master of Business Administration from the Indian Institute of Management at Lucknow.

1. Can you name a person who has had a tremendous impact on you as a leader? Why and how did this person impact your life?

My father has always inspired me in every walk of life. It is through his guidance and the trust he has reposed in me that I am where I am in my life today. In addition, the lessons of leadership he imparted to me were no different. Through him, I learnt various positive attributes, such as how a leader should treat his employees and how he should face challenges head-on. Furthermore, the importance of always looking at the future as well as the significance of taking everyone together along the path of growth and success.

2. What is one single characteristic that you believe every leader should possess?

A leader must be sensitive to the needs and aspirations of the people he is leading. Furthermore, he must never abandon them but, in fact, always attempt at all times to take them along on the business journey together.

3. What advice would you give someone going into a leadership position for the first time?

Always communicate with your fellow employees, and more importantly, should any problem arise, it is best to understand the same from the grass-roots level.

4. What's the most important leadership lesson you've learnt and how is it valuable?

Always look at the future of business and market and adapt yourself accordingly. Nuances and needs of business change every few years, so a leader needs to know in which direction to lead the business.

5. What accomplishment are you most proud of?

I am most proud of two of my achievements: The first has been to turn around Madhusudan Organics Ltd. from a sick unit to a company which is now well on its way to recover its past position in the industry. The second is the introduction of the Bitumen Trading Vertical within my organisation in the recent past.

6. What are you doing to ensure your continued growth and development as a leader?

In this case, I firmly believe in the importance of increasing efficiency in the existing business and always looking out for new opportunities

7. As an individual who has a busy professional life, how would you say your family contributed to your success?

Family has always played a very important role. They are the foundation of a leader. I have received immense support and guidance from my family. They have believed in me when things were tough and even today continue to enhance my confidence in my own abilities.

8. How do you keep your employees (or team members) keen and motivated?

I personally believe in making the employees feel that they own the company and the company is their own child. In the same way, the achievements of the company are also their personal achievements.

9. Social media today is an effective medium of communication. It can make or break the reputation of an organisation as well as its leader. How would you advise a leader should approach the transmission of his or her organisation's brand over this medium?

Social media is a double-edged sword that one must handle with extreme caution. It can make your company famous very fast, and at the same time, a single mistake can take it all away. Therefore, it important to be careful about what you put out there, and should the need arise, it is essential to not hesitate to take professional help as and when needed.

10. What steps are taken within the organisation to discover new leadership within your organisation? How would you go about preparing the individual for his/her future role?

Let employees take decisions. Even when they are wrong, stand by them and help them learn from those mistakes. Communicate with them on a regular basis. Give them full opportunity to hold the fort when you are away.

Bharat Bagla

Bees Network Limited
Financial Advisor

Bharat Bagla can be best described as a leader who wears many feathers in his cap. After a turbulent start to his education, which saw him going through five different schools, he finally passed out from the Bombay Cambridge School. After this, he completed his graduation at Narsee Monjee College of Commerce and Economics, Mumbai. He then further went out to gain a post-graduation from Manipal Academy of Higher Education. In the year 2007, he started out on his own and successfully set up sub-broking services to become the biggest franchisee of Reliance Money. He has been acknowledged as one of the leading and fastest-growing independent financial advisors both from East India as well as pan India. He has been an active member of Merchants' Chamber of Commerce as well as the Foundation of Independent Financial Advisors. He is a fitness enthusiast and has taken part in over 50 marathons in different parts of the globe.

1. Can you name a person who has had a tremendous impact on you as a leader? Why and how did this person impact your life?

One person who has had a tremendous impact on me is the character from a movie called 'Forrest Gump'. The character of Forrest Gump was portrayed by Tom Hanks in the movie. This character somehow moved a couple of strings inside me. Whenever I encounter a problem or I'm stuck in a situation, I refer to this movie to inspire me to find a solution to the problem at hand. In the movie, Forrest Gump is considered a not so intelligent man but has tremendous persistence capabilities and also is extremely hard-working, focused and relentless. These qualities demonstrated by Forrest Gump have greatly inspired me and also played a significant role in shaping me as a person.

2. What is one single characteristic that you believe every leader should possess?

It would not be easy to highlight just one characteristic. However, every leader should possess clarity of vision and thought. And most importantly, the leader must have a conviction in his own ideas and, above all else, also have the ability to dream.

3. What advice would you give someone going into a leadership position for the first time?

Today we live in a world of competence and efficiencies, which needs agility and adaptability. Hence, I would advise anyone getting into a leadership position for the first time to always remember to be flexible, be able to adapt to frequently changing environments and have a dominant expertise that is better than the others.

4. What's the most important leadership lesson you've learnt and how is it valuable?

An incident involving a government agency sometime back taught me perhaps the most valuable lessons. Such was the impact of this incident that it taught me many leadership lessons at one go. While I would not go into details, I can share with you the lessons it taught me. First, it taught me that anything is possible; therefore, it is essential to be confident. Second, never to live in preconceived notions, be flexible. Third, the importance of thinking out of the box can bring dramatic results, be creative. Fourth, it is vital to always empower yourself in any circumstances, be proactive. Fifth, it taught me to never feel stuck, and be adventurous. And finally, I also learnt not to feel inferior in any circumstance; in fact, being bold and courageous will always bring about better results.

5. What accomplishment are you most proud of?

After humble beginnings, I am proud to say that my company Bees Network Limited is currently among the top five Independent Financial Advisors in the city of Kolkata. Furthermore, we are among the top 125 Independent Financial Advisors in India.

6. What are you doing to ensure your continued growth and development as a leader?

One of the things that I'm doing to ensure my continued growth and development as a leader is to constantly update and upgrade myself on a regular basis. I try to read up as much as I can on a regular basis along with enrolling myself into various training and leadership development programmes to help upgrade my skills. Recently, I attended a programme at the Indian School of Business, Hyderabad.

7. As an individual who has a busy professional life, how would you say your family contributed to your success?

Professional success cannot be achieved without support from one's family. I have been blessed with a very loving, caring and encouraging family. They keep pushing me to pursue more and more while at the same time appreciate what I have achieved. They, at times, also critically advise me where necessary. In fact, the satisfaction one gets with having such a family is extremely motivating and pushes one to achieve higher and greater goals. My family has always stood by me in every situation and circumstance. As a typical day for me starts very early and often ends very late, I make it a point to catch up with all family affairs on Sundays and spend quality time with each and every member of my family on that day.

8. How do you keep your employees (or team members) keen and motivated?

We very strongly believe in investing time in upgrading and improving the lifestyle of our employees. Instead of rewarding them with a cash incentive, we keep finding innovative ways of surprising them with gifts that help them improve their overall lifestyle.

9. Social media today is an effective medium of communication. It can make or break the reputation of an organisation as well as its leader. How would you advise a leader should approach the transmission of his or her organisation's brand over this medium?

Social media today is like the tiger in the jungle. Once you decide to sit on it, you can't get off it. The dilemma is that if you don't sit on the tiger, the tiger will anyways kill you. Such is social media today that you cannot do without it, and neither can you effectively control it. One has to have a very well thought out strategy in place beforehand on how to engage social media for the organisation's communication to the outside world. A balanced approach has to be adopted while handling social media. Excessive exposure can be rewarding as well as destructive.

10. What steps are taken within the organisation to discover new leadership within your organisation? How would you go about preparing the individual for his/her future role?

Ours is a first-generation organisation, and we're still to formulate a succession strategy for us. Presently, we are unable to comment on this topic. However, we are actively thinking in this direction and are confident that we shall be able to put an appropriate plan in place in the coming years.

Anuj Madan

Chicky Madan Catering
Owner

Anuj Madan is a young and dynamic leader in the food and beverage industry. A third-generation businessman, he owns and manages the exceptionally successful catering business by the name of Chicky Madan Catering. This organisation proudly bears the name of its founder and was established in the year 1945. It has a formidable reputation for its culinary excellence, personal service and value for money. Anuj perfected his skills in the art of hospitality at the Taj Group of Hotels before joining his family business. He also holds an honours degree from the University of Huddersfield.

1. Can you name a person who has had a tremendous impact on you as a leader? Why and how did this person impact your life?

As a teenager, I always loved to watch the show 'Shark Tank'. One of the main investors (shark) on that show was the American businessman Mark Cuban. Other than his regular businesses, he's largely renowned as the owner of the Dallas Mavericks, a leading basketball team in the

National Basketball Association (NBA). Mark Cuban, through this show, left a positive impression on me, and I am motivated and encouraged to be a shark like him. His ability to convert a new start-up into a grand successful business continues to inspire me in my business even today.

2. What is one single characteristic that you believe every leader should possess?
In my opinion, perhaps the most crucial characteristics a leader should possess are motivational skills and also the ability to constantly innovate. Only with these essential attributes will a leader be in a position to yield the maximum benefits for himself, his employees and his organisation.

3. What advice would you give someone going into a leadership position for the first time?
My advice to upcoming leaders is to recognise that your colleagues and subordinates are your biggest assets. Identify the good ones within your organisation and simply don't let them go, as they will be the ones who will be responsible for your success in the future.

4. What's the most important leadership lesson you've learnt and how is it valuable?
This one motto has always helped me to maintain quality, which, in turn, has resulted in happy customers. It is: 'Digest what you can eat; never overtrade'.

5. What accomplishment are you most proud of?
Being from the food industry, I would say there is not just one accomplishment but a sum total of many accomplishments which makes a successful brand, and for me, being invited to cater to the best parties in town is the epitome of success.

6. What are you doing to ensure your continued growth and development as a leader?
As a leader, if you can maintain certain parameters such as quality control and delivering on your promises and commitments, then you have accomplished it all. Furthermore, if your work creates a legacy

that inspires others to dream more, learn more, do more and become more, then you are an excellent leader.

7. As an individual who has a busy professional life, how would you say your family contributed to your success?

My family is my backbone, and they have played a big role in where I am today. My guru and guide, my elder brother, always told me just one thing: never stop dreaming for the universe, only then will you get the world.

8. How do you keep your employees (or team members) keen and motivated?

No person will make a great leader if they want to do it all by themselves or take all the credit for themselves. My employees are my biggest assets, and as such, I treat them as my family and co-owners. In this way, I believe each and every one of them is a leader in their own way. This, I believe, goes a long way in keeping them motivated to give their best for the organisation time and time again.

9. Social media today is an effective medium of communication. It can make or break the reputation of an organisation as well as its leader. How would you advise a leader should approach the transmission of his or her organisation's brand over this medium?

Social media is very important, but I personally feel too much of it ruins the brand's exclusivity. So, a leader has to really keep this in mind and try to maintain a balance when using this platform for any sort of communication about their organisation.

10. What steps are taken within the organisation to discover new leadership within your organisation? How would you go about preparing the individual for his/her future role?

I firmly believe that leaders are not born, they are made. And within my organisation, I myself would need to create them. In simple terms, delegating work automatically creates a sense of responsibility, which I am confident will help my employees reach great heights in the future.

Behnaz Bulsara Dugar

Flash Fitness
Owner

Behnaz Bulsara Dugar began her journey in the world of business at the young age of 22 years, when she took over her family business, Adams Motor Works, located in the city of Kolkata. She, on her part, attended several service and technical examinations held by Maruti Udyog Limited. This, in turn, allowed her to understand and grow the business better. Her sincere and honest hard work was appreciated by Maruti, and in recognition of her efforts, she was the recipient of many awards and accolades in the category of customer care and satisfaction.

In 2012, she changed her profession and got certified to teach Zumba (an exercise fitness program which inculcates dance and aerobic movements to pulsating and fast music). She currently holds international licences to teach Zumba programmes to all age groups. She then established her own dance fitness company called Flash Fitness, a part of BVS Studios (Pvt) Ltd. Today she and the organisation created by her provide quality dance and fitness training throughout the year at multiple locations within the city of Kolkata.

1. Can you name a person who has had a tremendous impact on you as a leader? Why and how did this person impact your life?

There are two people who have had a tremendous impact on my leadership skills. The first was my late father, through whom I understood important values such as humanity. The second lesson was to give a patient hearing to all the problems of both customers and employees alike and not to rest until their problems or difficulties have been resolved. The other person is my husband, who I credit with teaching me almost everything that I know today and making me worldly-wise. I can sincerely say that his influence can be clearly seen in all aspects of my business, whether that is the importance of being smart in business, team building or even working with good and truthful people.

2. What is one single characteristic that you believe every leader should possess?

The fitness industry is a very competitive business. Almost everyone is selling a similar product or service. It is important how you, as a leader, create and make it different and interesting each time so that your client never gets bored and keeps coming back to you. Therefore, the key in our business is continuously innovating and creating different products, which helps to retain our old patrons and, at the same time, attract newer clients as well.

3. What advice would you give someone going into a leadership position for the first time?

I would advise them to have a strong set of rules and systems in place. Do not try and do everything yourself. And more importantly, focus on hiring good and responsible people who are able to follow these systems for you and keep a responsible watch on the day to day functioning of the organisation.

4. What's the most important leadership lesson you've learnt and how is it valuable?

Be fair to your employees and your clients. Understand a situation before making a decision. And at all times, try and resolve all issues peacefully.

5. What accomplishment are you most proud of?

There are two accomplishments which I am most proud to mention here. The first is that I was fortunate to be one of the first to host and promote Zumba certified training in the state of West Bengal in association with the Lead Zes of India, Sucheta Pal, thereby giving an opportunity to several other persons to get certified in their own right throughout the country.

The second is the creation of a unique self-defence programme designed by myself and my team, which is based on a mix of four martial arts—Japanese Karate, Chinese Kung Fu, Korean foot fighting art called Taekyon and also Muay Thai, the traditional martial art of Thailand. Furthermore, I was able to introduce this unique programme successfully at various schools, NGOs and clubs so as to empower women who travel unaccompanied for college, work and leisure activities.

6. What are you doing to ensure your continued growth and development as a leader?

I regularly update myself with Latest Zumba Instructor Network or 'ZIN' volumes every month. I identify what's trending in my industry. Furthermore, when I travel to a different country, I make it a point to visit their activity centres so as to see for myself what is trending with children and adults. I try and incorporate those ideas here in our classes, events and musicals accordingly.

7. As an individual who has a busy professional life, how would you say your family contributed to your success?

I am lucky to have a very supportive family. I started Flash Fitness when my daughter was six and my son, three years. My hours were long as our first class began at 7.30 am and the last one ended at 9 pm. Some days were extremely hectic for me. My mother has been a huge pillar of support as she has invested all her time and energy in raising my children. My husband has always got my back at work as well as at home. He continues to be a great support to us in more ways than one. In fact, even my in-laws have always encouraged me to follow my dreams and have supported me in every possible way.

8. How do you keep your employees (or team members) keen and motivated?

We at Flash Fitness are one big family, and as such, we regularly make an effort to plan events every other week, special classes, rewards, prizes, fun and games, boot camps, challenges and even invite outstation artists to conduct various workshops for us in their unique and different styles.

9. Social media today is an effective medium of communication. It can make or break the reputation of an organisation as well as its leader. How would you advise a leader should approach the transmission of his or her organisation's brand over this medium?

Social media can be used to create awareness, and it is a great tool to promote your work and organisation. More importantly, it should be used as a positive and effective instrument for feedback, which can help in improving the services of an organisation.

10. What steps are taken within the organisation to discover new leadership within your organisation? How would you go about preparing the individual for his/her future role?

Choose the people you work with wisely. It is best to give them small jobs initially so as to understand their depth and capability. Once you are satisfied with their ability, get them more involved and increase the amount of work as well as the incentives available to them. It is essential to form a team with the people you can trust and depend on in times of need. Always remember that it is the good people who always remain with you in the long term. So, choose them carefully and empower them to assist you in making your business function properly and efficiently.

Siddhartha Karnany

S M Ice Cream Mart
Owner

Siddharth Karnany is the perfect example of a quintessential family man who is also a business entrepreneur. His business career began almost as soon as he was out of college when he set up Eastern India's first ice-cream cone plant in the year 1996. Through his sincere hard work and foresight, he and his company today serve over 100 organisations within the competitive ice-cream industry. His main area of expertise and focus is in providing innovative packaging and production solution to his industry. Most recently, his organisation has diversified into many fields such as plastic, horticulture, packaging and food chemicals. Furthermore, many in his industry believe that he and his organisation are well on their way to becoming one of the major players in the ice-cream industry in the near future.

1. Can you name a person who has had a tremendous impact on you as a leader? Why and how did this person impact your life?

I credit my transformation into a leader to Mr G. K. Tandon, a business coach who I had the chance of meeting in the year 2014. It was his guidance and direction that allowed me to discover and implement a system which showed me a clear path to transform the scale of my business from a small enterprise to a larger, more successful organisation. Furthermore, I am also greatly inspired by businessmen such as Azim Premji and Rahul Bajaj, who are great examples of larger-than-life figures who provide world-class products at affordable prices throughout our country as well as abroad.

2. What is one single characteristic that you believe every leader should possess?

I would advise them to cultivate the habit of honesty. Be honest not only to yourself, your organisation and your clients but also to everyone around you. Honesty will build your character and will greatly reflect on the character of your organisation. In fact, it is only through honesty that people will trust you and, in turn, support you in your business.

3. What advice would you give someone going into a leadership position for the first time?

Always have a plan in place. Circumstances are not in our control, but the plan is. We might have to make changes along the way for the plan to work, but it is essential to stick to the plan as and how it was initially conceived. Be patient as nothing will happen overnight. Work hard and be passionate and you will surely achieve your goals. Furthermore, and more importantly, 90% of the people you meet will discourage you from your plans and abilities. Ignore them and all their reasons for why it won't work, and believe the one reason why you and your plans will succeed. Give it your best shot and be assured that your success may come late, but it will surely come.

4. What's the most important leadership lesson you've learnt and how is it valuable?

It is important to invest in top-quality people. It is essential to appoint qualified and experienced employees. Spend time in training them and align them to your and the organisation's vision and goals. From the top management to the lowest employee, all should be made to feel that they are part of the organisation and that their contribution is helping the company to grow. If you take good care of your people, rest assured that they will give their best for you and the organisation.

5. What accomplishment are you most proud of?

We have many firsts under our belt such as:

1st company to manufacture ice-cream cones in Eastern India – Year 1996

1st company to manufacture cream wafer biscuits in Eastern India – Year 1999

1st company to manufacture canapes in Eastern India – Year 2007

1st company to manufacture rolled sugar cones in Eastern India – Year 2017

But the one accomplishment that I am most proud of came in the year 2013, when we realised that we can be a notable brand in our space of work and have a substantial influence in the field of ice cream and other allied products.

6. What are you doing to ensure your continued growth and development as a leader?

I firmly believe this: "My competition is with myself, and I see how I can be a better person today than I was yesterday". To this effect, I am a voracious reader of inspirational and motivational stories of successful people who made odd situations favourable for themselves. I am also an extrovert and enjoy meeting and interacting with new people so that I can expand my knowledge in other subjects and disciplines of life. Currently, I am working on transforming myself to become a good listener.

7. As an individual who has a busy professional life, how would you say your family contributed to your success?

My family is my support system, and I believe that it is important to be with them in each and every step of life. I highly recommend everyone to share the problem they face at the workspace with their family so that they can understand the same and also are aware of the situation which exists. Both my parents have showered me with great love and support and have been of immense help in my personal and professional life. My wife is my constant support and stands by me in my every decision. One of her greatest contributions to my success is that she has taken over the responsibilities of the home so as to allow me to maintain my focus at work.

8. How do you keep your employees (or team members) keen and motivated?

It is always important for an organisation to have motivated and sincere working employees. The easiest way to achieve this is to involve them in regular discussions on the development of the product as well as other implementation processes. It is a great advantage to listen to their ideas and appreciate the same. In fact, one should always appreciate the hard work put in by them and acknowledge and encourage their participation at all levels within the workspace.

9. Social media today is an effective medium of communication. It can make or break the reputation of an organisation as well as its leader. How would you advise a leader should approach the transmission of his or her organisation's brand over this medium?

Social media is an important medium which should be utilised to advertise one's service and brand to millions of users. It is also one of the key mediums where a brand can understand the requirement of the masses and address the same. However, on a personal note, I would say that it reduces the valuable time available to an individual, which they should utilise in focusing on their work. Therefore, I recommend that we should all try and achieve a balance and curtail the time which is spent on social media in general.

10. What steps are taken within the organisation to discover new leadership within your organisation? How would you go about preparing the individual for his/her future role?

It is very important for the organisation to discover new leadership within the workplace. Here's one of the practices we have adopted within our organisation to deal with our workers: Every 15 days, we split the workers into small groups of 6 to 10 and allocate the leadership role to one of them. In our experience, over a period of time, almost all the workers have a chance to experience that role. We, on our part, are able to review and gauge the performance of each worker on an individual basis. The best performers are identified and are given a chance to begin the second level of training in other aspects of our organisation. Since this method has been introduced in the year 2013, we have successfully identified eight such workers, who have now moved up to the managerial level. We then consequently introduced the system at the higher levels of the organisation and have achieved excellent results.

Anindya Mandal

Ruby Financial Services
Director

Anindya Mandal is best described as a financial maverick with a heart of gold. He discovered his entrepreneurial streak while he was still in school and yet to appear for his class 10 board exams. His first venture was a shop which offered office automation services such as photocopying, stationery and even a courier service. While this venture was small in nature, it was to set the foundation stones for his entry into the financial business. It was his regular trips to procure the items from the Dalhousie area in Kolkata and the close proximity of its location to the Calcutta Stock Exchange which fuelled an intense desire in him to enter the financial services business. He thus began the selling of financial instruments, and as per his own admission, his first clients were his family members and close friends. Today Anindya Mandal and Ruby Financial Services, the company he founded in the year 1997, are regarded as one of the premier independent financial advisors in the whole country.

1. Can you name a person who has had a tremendous impact on you as a leader? Why and how did this person impact your life?

It was my father who tremendously influenced me in my role as a leader. He came from a humble background and in the initial years dedicated himself to flourish his 200-year-old family business of fish farming. He further diversified into the film exhibition business with the inauguration of Bunty Cinema, the biggest cinema hall in the city of Kolkata. He was also a smart investor in his own right, having acquired a large portfolio of real estate property, which provided a handsome return on his investment but also provided him with an opportunity to earn a substantial profit from the rent that was generated from these properties. He was well placed and respected in society and also served as a board of director of Eastern Motion Pictures Association as well as an honorary dignitary of Film Federation of India. He continues to remain an inspiration to me even today.

2. What is one single characteristic that you believe every leader should possess?

A leader must always be a good listener. He must make it his habit to completely listen and understand all the points in a conversation. Once the conversation has ended, a leader must take time to then analyse all the possible and relevant parts and then must decide on the best course of action.

3. What advice would you give someone going into a leadership position for the first time?

In my experience, leaders must inculcate into their persona the virtue of patience so that they can wait for the correct time to make the correct move. And second, they must practice tolerance when dealing with their subordinates. In fact, I strongly believe that taking a 24-hour break to reflect over an important decision has always held me in good stead. It is better to delay an important decision than to make one in haste.

4. What's the most important leadership lesson you've learnt and how is it valuable?

I must confess that in the early part of my career, I was not a good listener. I had the habit of talking more than I should have and that too from an authoritative point of view. It was the good advice from my father which allowed me to change this habit, and I began the practice of deliberately not being the first one to speak, and only when others had completed their say would I then offer my point of view. I can tell you with great confidence that this system has served me well. Half of the problem got sorted immediately, and the other half of the problem got solved through the solutions offered by the others who were part of the conversation.

5. What accomplishment are you most proud of?

I am a proud son of Bengal, and my proudest moment is winning the CNBC Financial Advisors Awards for four consecutive years in a row in various categories, which reflects the excellence of service that we provide to our customers and clientele.

6. What are you doing to ensure your continued growth and development as a leader?

I believe it is my duty to provide a healthy working environment for my employees. Special care is taken to review their performance, and they receive appropriate incentives as per their ability and potential. We also offer our employees generous medical benefits for themselves and their families. Furthermore, we take pride in assuring tangible and safe retirement benefits for their secure future.

7. As an individual who has a busy professional life, how would you say your family contributed to your success?

According to me, a leader's most vital quality is to keep themselves free so that they are always in a position to monitor everybody else's progress. As and when the situation requires, he or she should be in a position to intervene and set what is required back on course. As for my family, they are my number one priority. It is a good practice to set up the administration of a business such that the organisation is able to function by itself. I have put in just such a system, and it provides me with extra time to spend with my family. For me, it is my family which is the biggest and strongest support in all my endeavours. Thus, whenever there is any spare time available, I prefer spending it with my family.

8. How do you keep your employees (or team members) keen and motivated?

I believe in the phrase "Family First" and encourage the same to be followed within my organisation. I don't let any of my employees work when there is a problem in their family; in fact, there have been many times when I have sent that person home, and leave is granted till the problem is solved. This is because I believe that a person with a disturbed mind cannot give his 100% at the workplace. Furthermore, I feel that taking at least one holiday in a year with family is very necessary for a healthy life. Therefore, I insist that each of my employees takes travel leave once every year, and I add some free incentives which can be enjoyed by their respective family members as well.

9. Social media today is an effective medium of communication. It can make or break the reputation of an organisation as well as its leader. How would you advise a leader should approach the transmission of his or her organisation's brand over this medium?

I will agree to a certain extent that social media is an effective means of communication and does allow the opportunity for an organisation to be recognised as a brand. However, in our line of work, maintaining a personal touch with the client is an essential need and requirement. In my personal experience, I would say that it is the personalised service that we as an organisation have provided to our clients which has played a great part in the strong growth of the business.

10. What steps are taken within the organisation to discover new leadership within your organisation? How would you go about preparing the individual for his/her future role?

I, on my part, have already initiated the process of introducing the next generation, which includes even the children of my existing employees. Before inducting them, I personally brief them on what is expected from them and provide them with a clear idea of their job role within the organisation. On my part, I keep a strict vigil on their performance, and as and when they start achieving each milestone, I further encourage them through an increase in their salary and also reward them with tangible incentives. Those of them who perform the best over a long period of time will most definitely find a permanent position within the organisation.

Atul Makharia

Speed Group of Companies
Director

Atul Makharia has always been a motorsport enthusiast and is perhaps a perfect example of an individual who followed a passion which he later turned into a successful and flourishing business. His career spans over 20 years and has been solely dedicated to the automobile industry. His enthusiasm has resulted in his implementing leading large-scale projects from inception to their eventual completion. His creation of the Speed Group within the city of Kolkata encompasses some of the most popular and trustworthy brands both in India as well as from around the world in the motorcycle industry, such as Piaggio India, Kawasaki India, Harley-Davidson India and BMW Motorrad. By his own admission, he strives to establish and maintain the quality, safety as well as financial operational standards to a global scale so as to produce positive impacts on the overall performance of his organisation.

1. Can you name a person who has had a tremendous impact on you as a leader? Why and how did this person impact your life?

I credit Grand Master Choa Kok Sui, who completely changed my view about the world. His teachings have guided and inspired me in all facets of my life and continue to do so even today. I would recommend to any new leader to realise that in life as well as in our professional life, many of us do not have a clear idea of what exactly we wish to achieve; therefore, it is important to have well-defined goals in place. Also, even if the goals are clear, we have no clear plan on how to go about achieving them. Therefore, it is essential to realise that both selecting and achieving the goal in our life will present us with various challenges, and it is best to realise that all these challenges serve the purpose of educating us and expanding our thought processes. Therefore, welcome the challenges in the workplace and learn from them.

2. What is one single characteristic that you believe every leader should possess?

I believe that it is essential for any leader to possess the ability to observe without judgement and listen without any prejudice. Only by adopting these practices will a leader be in a position to act as a mentor and guide within his own organisation.

3. What advice would you give someone going into a leadership position for the first time?

I would advise them to take the time to observe and understand the surroundings of their workplace and then, to their best ability, create a happy working environment for all of their employees. Furthermore, a leader must inculcate in themselves the habit of speaking to the point, and all their communication must be clear and precise so that their message can be understood easily by all the persons with whom they interact.

4. What's the most important leadership lesson you've learnt and how is it valuable?

The most important lesson in leadership is to realise the importance of teamwork. Behind the success of any leader, you will find a group of individuals who work together in a united and target-oriented team. Therefore, it is essential to build and create a team within your workforce who share your core values and believe in your aspirations. Furthermore, when you are able to identify people with this type of dedication, make all the effort to see that they never leave you or your organisation.

5. What accomplishment are you most proud of?

The award for the best dealer for Harley-Davidson in India for the year 2017 remains the accomplishment I am most proud of till date.

6. What are you doing to ensure your continued growth and development as a leader?

I hold regular one-on-one meetings with my team members at our different locations around the city of Kolkata. I encourage them to share their suggestions and ideas for the improvement of our organisation. From what is presented, the best suggestions are implemented. These meetings allow me to grow as a leader and improve my problem-solving abilities as well as allow me to identify and retain the best people for the growth and development of my organisation.

7. As an individual who has a busy professional life, how would you say your family contributed to your success?

I am blessed to have a very supportive family. It is much to their credit that I am able to give my 100% at my work from Monday to Friday. However, my family also insists that I must give them 100% of my attention on the weekends, that is Saturday and Sunday. Nonetheless, if there is an urgent and pressing family matter, I make it a point to be present, and they always have my support.

8. How do you keep your employees (or team members) keen and motivated?

I believe in maintaining a small core group of people who are highly paid for their service to the organisation. Furthermore, I encourage an open and fair atmosphere, where all matters can be discussed openly and honestly. Each member of my team is instructed to help one another to solve both professional and personal problems so that it encourages stronger bonds and relationships within them. This small practice translates to a happy and tranquil environment within the workspace.

9. Social media today is an effective medium of communication. It can make or break the reputation of an organisation as well as its leader. How would you advise a leader should approach the transmission of his or her organisation's brand over this medium?

Social media can be both a blessing and a curse for an organisation. On my part, I use it as an effective medium to receive feedback from our customers. In cases where I have received negative feedback, I personally intervene to resolve the issue quickly, amicably and to the utmost satisfaction of my customers.

10. What steps are taken within the organisation to discover new leadership within your organisation? How would you go about preparing the individual for his/her future role?

I always try and promote from within my organisation. Any new employees in the organisation are always introduced at the lower level and will have to work their way to the top. This open and fair system, which recognises and rewards an employee for their good work, keeps the team always motivated to give their best for our organisation.

Vinay Bamalwa

Nemichand Bamalwa Jewellers
Director

Vinay Bamalwa comes from a long line of successful and distinguished business leaders. He plays an active part in managing the operations of Nemichand Bamalwa & Sons, one of the leading jewellers of India. Nemichand Bamalwa & Sons is a traditionally run family business engaged in the jewellery industry and boasts of being over 100 years old. Their primary business is retailing their products through their existing showrooms located at many prominent locations within the city of Kolkata as well as around India. Furthermore, the organisation operates within a wide range of activities from manufacturing, retailing and wholesale to import and export.

1. Can you name a person who has had a tremendous impact on you as a leader? Why and how did this person impact your life?

One becomes a leader not by following just one person but by modelling multiple areas of excellence demonstrated by a multitude of people. I have been lucky that the people who have impacted me the most are my family members. Let me explain it in this way: I am inspired by the no-compromise approach of my uncle Mr Madanlal Bamalwa; I am equally impressed by the humane nature of my father, Mr Hansraj Bamalwa; My uncle Bachhraj Bamalwa is very detail-oriented, and my younger uncle Mr Bajrang Bamalwa has the ability of binding people. All these individuals have shaped my life. Furthermore, as I have grown up in a family business, I have great reverence towards my father for the sheer respect and admiration he has in the eyes of his company's stakeholders. They have all played a great part in shaping me into the confident and capable person who is able to manage our large organisation.

2. What is one single characteristic that you believe every leader should possess?

I am well aware that the success of any organisation rests on its leaders. Therefore, it is the duty of the present leader in an organisation to have the innate ability to create more future leaders. In this way, it becomes possible for an organisation to continue and grow for generations.

3. What advice would you give someone going into a leadership position for the first time?

I would advise them to first spend adequate time to understand the main ethos of the organisation and make a sincere effort to bond and foster a relationship with their colleagues and co-workers. Secondly and perhaps more importantly, to consider themselves not as a boss but, more appropriately, as a catalyst that makes others shine such that even in a situation where you may have done the job entirely by yourself, you must make it a point to share the credit with your staff and employees.

4. What's the most important leadership lesson you've learnt and how is it valuable?

The most valuable lesson would be to remain flexible in the workplace. If an individual remains flexible enough, they will be open to trying multiple ways of solving a problem. It is also the flexibility in relationships that will allow them to win the hearts and minds of all who they will encounter, whether that is employees or customers. Only through the winning of these hearts can a leader expect greater commitment and dedication from them.

5. What accomplishment are you most proud of?

That accomplishment would be the creation of a division from scratch and also the attainment of good revenue in a relatively short period of time. This was a specially rewarding achievement as I had zero experience in that particular line of work.

6. What are you doing to ensure your continued growth and development as a leader?

I keep an open mind and inculcate the good attributes of others by observing them. I am also a voracious reader and set out time so as to enable myself to attend various workshops/seminars on self-development.

7. As an individual who has a busy professional life, how would you say your family contributed to your success?

I will simply say that my family has contributed immensely; they are the cornerstone of my success, as I work for my family.

8. How do you keep your employees (or team members) keen and motivated?

Within my organisation, I make it a point to respect each and every one of my employees and co-workers. I allow them opportunities to improve themselves by promoting learning on the job. As and when they perform well, I make it a point to see that they receive the appropriate recognition. Furthermore, it is my endeavour to create a harmonious working environment within my organisation.

9. Social media today is an effective medium of communication. It can make or break the reputation of an organisation as well as its leader. How would you advise a leader should approach the transmission of his or her organisation's brand over this medium?

Consistent visibility on social media is the necessity of the day. All organisations should be careful about what kind of message they are communicating on this platform. In my opinion, it is best to remain understated yet bold in the selection of messages when using such mediums.

10. What steps are taken within the organisation to discover new leadership within your organisation? How would you go about preparing the individual for his/her future role?

I believe in encouraging initiatives where there is freedom to succeed and fail also. Implementing the concept of Failure = Learning to adopt various methods to succeed. Furthermore, I provide constant support and mentoring to all persons associated with my organisation.

Vandita Sanghvi

Curious Little
Director

Vandita Sanghvi is the creative and innovative owner of Curious Little, an activity centre for children located in the city of Kolkata. Her organisation offers a unique environment where children are encouraged to create, imagine, learn and grow. She and her team of highly motivated and dedicated individuals are constantly updating themselves to remain at par with the newer aspects of children's growth and development on a global basis. In her own words, her motivation has never been money but more a labour of love, and her only endeavour is to support her team and the children she instructs and educates to always stay curious! Her own children are her inspiration; they not only keep her well-grounded but are a constant reminder that there yet remains so much in the world to read, know and learn. She also holds a master's in advertising and marketing from The University of Leeds.

1. Can you name a person who has had a tremendous impact on you as a leader? Why and how did this person impact your life?

I would like to attribute my success to my father. During my early years, he sowed the seeds of independence in me. He allowed me to be a free spirit, to explore out anything and everything (of course, within set limits), encouraged me to read and explore and made me travel the world. What truly stood out was that he provided me with every opportunity to improve myself and always treated me equally and at par in all aspects of my life. He consciously encouraged me to think for myself and taught me to be accountable for my actions.

2. What is one single characteristic that you believe every leader should possess?

Humility is what I believe is the most essential characteristic. A great leader is one who agrees to the fact that they do not 'know it all'. No individual in this world has become a leader on just their own accord. Without a support system, success is hard to come by. A leader should be a team player and, most importantly, acknowledge the people around him or her.

3. What advice would you give someone going into a leadership position for the first time?

Always be ready to learn and educate. If you stop learning, you stop growing. Complacency and arrogance are nothing short of a death knell. A good leader is one who understands that you cannot do everything on your own. Furthermore, by educating others, you can delegate some responsibilities to them, thereby allowing the people working under you to grow and, in turn, allow you some precious free time for yourself to focus, innovate and introduce newer ideas in your organisation.

4. What's the most important leadership lesson you've learnt and how is it valuable?

Success has many fathers—but remaining true to yourself and the people who are part of your journey is more important than those who attach themselves to you after you are known.

5. What accomplishment are you most proud of?

I have been very humble at every stage of my life and am very grateful for all that I have managed to achieve through the guidance and encouragement of others, whether that be being chosen as the head girl of my school or being told I am doing such a wonderful job at bringing up my children. The one time I truly felt a sense of accomplishment is when someone came up to my father and asked him if he was Vandita's father. My father's reaction was what made me feel I had actually achieved something.

6. What are you doing to ensure your continued growth and development as a leader?

The maxim of my company is something I truly believe in: to stay curious. I endeavour to learn, read and travel as much as I possibly can. I am constantly on the lookout for courses which add value to the different facets of my life—be it work or my personality. I love attending symposiums by people from different fields of work, which allows me the opportunity to experience their different perspectives and implement positive changes in my life.

7. As an individual who has a busy professional life, how would you say your family contributed to your success?

Someone has rightfully said: "It takes a village to raise a child". My husband, my parents and my in-laws have helped me immensely by stepping in to take care of the children—picking them up from school or coordinating things for me. My mother is my sounding board, and I regularly discuss and seek out her advice on many matters. She, on her part, always encourages remaining patient and maintaining my calm composure when dealing with different situations on a day to day basis.

8. How do you keep your employees (or team members) keen and motivated?

Sharing a common vision with my team and then figuring out various methods by which the same may be achieved. The whole team is made to realise how they are an important cog in the wheel and how we would fail to achieve our collective goal without their positive contribution. This being said, they are made accountable and responsible, and I personally follow up with them at regular intervals of time.

9. Social media today is an effective medium of communication. It can make or break the reputation of an organisation as well as its leader. How would you advise a leader should approach the transmission his or his organisation's brand over this medium?

One has to take ownership of their actions on social media and be sensible. Sometimes you can gain valuable insight from the feedback that people give. However, you cannot do everything right. If an adverse situation arises, the leader should take stock and initiate action to set the situation right.

10. What steps are taken within the organisation to discover new leadership within your organisation? How would you go about preparing the individual for his/her future role?

A good leader is one who knows when to intervene and when to let the team be by itself. It is a good practice to assign responsibility, set a deadline and then let the team do the job the way they deem fit. At the same time, make yourself available when they need you and check in on their progress from time to time. Encourage innovation and give praise when and where deserved.

Lightning Source UK Ltd.
Milton Keynes UK
UKHW040236240919
350318UK00001B/170/P

9 781645 877387